CELEBRATING A *Life*

Commemorat

CELEBRATING A *Life*

Planning Memorial Services and Other Creative Remembrances

FAITH MOORE

Stewart, Tabori & Chang
New York

For my brother Johnny, who inspired this book.

CONTENTS

FOREWORD

There is so much *in*appropriate handling of death in today's world; it is a subject that yearned to be addressed. And this thoughtful guide does a thorough job of just that.

We've grown accustomed to creative new ways of celebrating marriage. Funky graduation fêtes, nontraditional baptismal rites, and outrageously glittery sweet sixteen parties are now the norm. Logically, there has been a growing desire, as well as a need, for new customs involving all of them, but with the rite of death in particular. So many of us lose any semblance of our *cool* when confronting someone's passage to the other side. We don't know what to say to the spouse or what actions to take to express our love and support for the family. We want to honor our loved one's memory, but perhaps all the options that immediately come to mind seem too cliché. How do you handle the rude creatures who are pressing for details of the deceased's estate? Do you serve food during this sad time, and if so, what, when, and to whom? There seem to be a million questions arising around the final act of someone's "leaving us." And Faith Moore answers a good many of them in the following pages.

As a writer on manners, it's easy for me to urge that all the players follow the established social rules in all the rituals of life. But many people today take great delight in breaking them. Of course, to that I say, "Fine, but what do you advise as substitute behavior?" At least know the customary protocol before straying from it.

Moore takes a fresh approach on the whole subject—walking us through the planning process, delving into the historical and sociological importance of the way we "do" funerals in America today, and offering some good, solid advice on the roles that family, friends, and associates should play in giving the deceased the proper "send-off." Yes, a memorial service can be looked upon as a celebration. Doing it properly, in my mind, is like mastering a great recipe. What is needed are first-class ingredients, loving care, and a healthy measure of heart.

— Letitia Baldrige

1

Why Settle for
Less Than Extraordinary?

When the curtain opened, a central spotlight shone brightly on a sparkling pair of silver sneakers, resting alone on the stark seat of a wooden chair. More than a thousand of the fashion industry's most prominent figures had gathered in Carnegie Hall, not for a show, but to remember and honor Kal Ruttenstein, one of the industry's most respected designers. His star rose when he introduced the world to rhinestone-studded jeans; his talent endured throughout his life. Everyone there recognized Kal's silver sneakers, a poignant reminder of the one person who could ever fill them. Their meaning was not lost on the audience. More than a fashion statement, they were a symbol of how people were paying attention to more than just the words spoken at the memorial service. They proved that the simplest touches could create an indelible memory.

Symbolism can take many forms. At another memorial service, in a town fifty miles south of San Diego, a woman by the name of Andrea stood in front of a much smaller gathering to celebrate the memory of her father. There were no celebrities in the audience; her father, while well known in town, was a man of modest means who chose to work with his hands, first as a builder then later as a handyman. Everyone recognized the oversized leather flight jacket Andrea was wearing. On chilly days her father was never without it. The jacket—like the silver shoes—was a touching reminder of the World War II veteran.

Not so long ago these simple symbols, chosen as a way of honoring a departed loved one, would have been considered in poor taste and out of place. A favorite daughter would have worn black, not her father's care-worn flight jacket. There was a proper way of doing things. But when the baby boomers came of age and began getting married, they started doing things their way. They began placing more emphasis on making weddings meaningful for themselves and their friends, and less on appeasing the wishes of their families. The youth of that generation rejected the traditions that meant nothing to them and kept the traditions they liked. They found different places to get married: by the sea, on a mountaintop, in a field, on a boat, on a tropical island, in a castle. The destination wedding became commonplace. People started dressing in ways that reflected their personalities, whether that meant going barefoot, sporting Hawaiian shirts and Bermuda shorts, or wearing a silk gown in a favorite shade of blue. Even black, once a symbol of disrespect, is now an acceptable color to wear to a wedding.

Reinventing wedding traditions was just the beginning. Soon after, a "party culture" evolved, raising the bar for extravagance for celebrations such as birthdays, graduations, and Bar and Bat Mitzvahs. It makes sense, then, that another important event—the funeral, or memorial service—would start to be treated in the same way. So, as three-quarters of a million baby boomers and the generations that follow are thrust, often for the first time, into planning memorial services, they are also reimagining how to say good-bye to the ones they love.

WHY THE TIME IS RIGHT FOR CHANGE

A party culture is one that is always looking to set a celebratory tone; for a memorial service this means being more inclined to focus on the positive aspects of a person's life rather than a public, prolonged mourning. Yet it is still important to acknowledge this life milestone, grieve as a community, and, even more importantly, lay a person to rest with respect, grace, and honor. More and more people no longer wish to leave the details and decision-making to someone else. They prefer to take control and do things their way. This has led to what can be called the "My Way Memorial Movement".

The many new ways people are choosing to remember loved ones demonstrate that the systems currently in place are insufficient. Even the euphemisms used to talk about those who have died—passed, passed on, passed away, deceased, expired (the correct medical term), gone to a better place, crossed over—seem inadequate. There is a stigma attached to the term "dead." In conversation we rarely say the "person who died" or the "dead person" because it sounds too harsh. A memorial service is a time to remember a person in their best light. It is for this reason that throughout this book I will refer to the person who has died as the *honoree*.

More people are taking the term "paying your respects" to heart and electing to have memorial services that acknowledge a person's life instead of focusing so intently on their death. In addition to having a more celebratory culture there are several other reasons for the trend. Memorial services are inherently open to a wider community of friends and acquaintances, often including people who come solely to support a grieving friend. And secondly, more people are choosing cremation or, even if opting for a traditional burial, deciding to hold a memorial ceremony without the body present, making it much easier to celebrate than grieve.

EXPLORING YOUR OPTIONS

According to recent reports from the National Center for Health Statistics, approximately 2.5 million people die per year in the United States, creating a funeral industry in the range of $13 billion. When people found they needed more support planning weddings, the wedding planner industry was born. In much the same way, the funeral industry is also experiencing a boom as people consider all the possible ways to hold a memorial service. You will find that providers in the industry are very aware of the trend toward personalization and are prepared and willing to work with you to help create the perfect event.

Just over sixteen percent of all people in the United States have no religious affiliation. There are many more who simply do not wish for a standard funeral service, which is often conducted by someone who does not know their family. Without the support of a religious institution, most people turn to the funeral industry to help with burial arrangements and an accompanying funeral or memorial service. While these services are respectful, they can also feel like a formality, a ritualistic way to say good-bye. There is little, if any, attention given to the small, personal touches that make a gathering special. The rituals performed are grounded in years of tradition, a sharp contrast to the celebratory nature of today's society.

As a growing number of people look for an alternative, a new industry is emerging. Secular celebrants are becoming an integral part of the funeral business. Although their main role is presiding over a service in place of a religious officiant, they are also an invaluable resource for funeral directors wanting to provide a more tailored experience for their clients.

Regardless of who leads you through the planning process or presides over the ceremony, a memorial service, first and foremost, should glorify the life of the honoree. People need the opportunity to grieve together, release their feelings, and recognize the value of the lives lived by those they love. For many, attending a "celebration of life" will feel more comforting and therapeutic than a traditional funeral.

WHY PLANS GO WRONG AND WHAT YOU CAN DO ABOUT IT

A common reaction of people faced with the task of planning a service, regardless of whether it is a simple family funeral or a large-scale memorial service, is to call on an outside source for help. In many ways this decision can be a good one, easing the burden of making arrangements in a time of grief. However, it can also lead to the loss of control over the planning, leading to an event swept in an unintended direction.

Edna died in her nineties, at home, surrounded by family. They had time to say good-bye and prepare for her death emotionally. But when she died, Edna's children arranged to hold her memorial service within the week. They called the Episcopalian church she had attended for many years and agreed upon a date and time. Yet when they met with the minister to discuss the service, they were unprepared for their reception. Rather than a sympathetic consoling figure, an overwrought, impatient man greeted them. There were too many weddings, too many christenings, too many funerals—far more work than what he had been led to believe when he agreed to fill in for a pastor on leave. The minister told the family exactly what the service would be: just the minimal funeral and no eulogy. They could not believe what they were hearing. This unanticipated response was so outlandish it was almost laughable. But the family had already placed the notice and had to move forward with the service they were handed.

While this is an extreme example of how a bereaved family can lose control of a memorial service, there are more subtle ways things can go wrong when plans are made under duress. Often there are extenuating circumstances, such as trying to make arrangements quickly or from a long distance, that contribute to the difficulty of establishing a meaningful ceremony. On the other hand, some people are too upset to make any decisions and are perfectly willing to hand the task over to someone else. Only later, when reflecting upon what happened, do they realize what might have been.

This book is not about regrets, but rather about learning how and why to plan and how to create a more memorable way to say good-bye. It is about making sure you and your loved ones are remembered in a way you and they would have wanted. It is also about second chances, and showing you how to re-celebrate the life of an honoree—especially when you feel the need for a more satisfying closure, an ongoing remembrance, or a way to include people who couldn't participate in the first service or ceremony.

THE IMPORTANCE OF PLANNING

As a professional event planner for more than twenty years, I have regularly been asked to help friends, family, and clients plan "the ultimate event," a thoughtful and creative memorial service. When asked about their memorial service, people often say that no one should make a fuss over them. Most people simply do not like to think about death, let alone talk about it.

One of the primary reasons for having a wedding is to create a memory for friends, family, and the couple, to earmark the transition from son and daughter to husband and wife. No other celebration is traditionally as elaborate or as festive. The next celebration that serves that same purpose, to acknowledge a major life transition, is the memorial service. On average, people have three days to plan a memorial service for a loved one. Weddings, on the other hand, can take months or even years to plan. Considering the importance of the event, there is no reason that a memorial service should not be planned in advance, just like a wedding.

In my office we often ask, "If you were hit by a bus tomorrow, would everyone be prepared to carry on without you?" Many people think they are finished planning once they've created a will. But, unless you have clearly written down guidelines for your memorial service, you cannot be sure your family will know how to fulfill your last wishes. Perhaps the service will be handed over to a clergy member who never knew you or anyone in your family. Maybe the burden of decision-making will rest with friends or family during a time when they need to grieve.

Planning ahead empowers the loved ones you leave behind. When somebody close to you dies, it is natural to feel like a victim of circumstance. After all, we have no control over the moment when death strikes. We can, however, choose how we celebrate that person's life. And regardless of how we choose to say good-bye, the experience is a necessary ritual for finding closure and peace of mind. When people celebrate the life of an honoree with dignity, guilt can subside. Think about how having a clear plan will release your loved ones from the frustration of wondering what your wishes would have been or—worse—feeling guilty for not intuitively knowing what you would have wanted.

Sometimes we simply don't know what our wishes are and need to make time to figure out what is important, what should be included, and what should be discarded. Planning will help you make the right decisions.

The first time you have to plan a service for someone who has left no wishes behind you will realize what a daunting task it can be. Where should you gather to celebrate? What tone should the service take? What music should you play? What words would best describe the honoree's character and accomplishments? Who are the most appropriate speakers?

On the flip side, once you realize that this is important and an opportunity to once again put your own creative stamp on a life milestone, you'll ask yourself, "Why settle for what others choose to do when we can plan something extraordinary?"

EXPRESSING YOUR WISHES

Creating your own service is all about doing something positive, something my sister believes in firmly. As an oncologist, she takes a traditional western approach to medicine (prescribing chemotherapy and proven drugs). However, when people come to her and say, "What about my sister-in-law who suggested avocado oil massages?" she will say, "Good, yes, you should do that and continue taking your medication. Try the avocado oil because whenever you feel you are doing something positive, you are doing something to help."

As you take time to plan and write down your wishes, you will gradually find it easier to think about, then talk about, and eventually maybe even laugh about your memorial service. As you consider different options, you might even become more adventurous about the context in which you would like people to remember you. Conversely, you might find that you want a more traditional service, but now know how to express what that means in a way that others will understand and easily implement.

When planning for yourself you never know how much time you have, so the earlier you start thinking and planning, the better. Keep a file of clippings, favorite music, and quotations that resonate with you. Ponder the questions posed in this book. Write down your wishes and entrust them to a loved one who will carry them out.

LESS IS MORE

In the following pages you'll find guidance on every component of planning. Even if you have only a few days to make arrangements, this book will provide you with numerous ways to quickly and inexpensively create a fulfilling, celebratory memorial service. When considering all of these ideas, you might be tempted to create a service that goes over the top. The true intent of this book is to help you create a memorial service that is true to the wishes of the honoree and provides guests the satisfaction of participating in a proper send-off. We have all heard the slogan, "Less is more." A memorial service is the perfect occasion to follow that rule. Just one thoughtful touch, embellishment, or change in venue can turn an impersonal, ordinary service into one that is truly extraordinary.

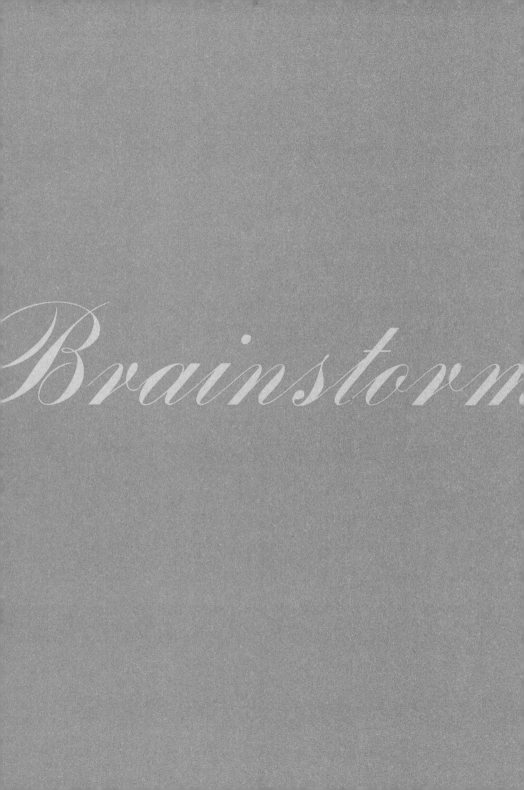

2
Three Questions
for Creative Planning

Planning ahead helps you ensure that your memorial service captures your essence and offers comfort to those who attend. You are creating a portrait of yourself that will be enormously helpful to those left behind. This is an ongoing process, one that you should revisit every few years as your preferences evolve.

The first step in answering the three questions presented in this chapter is to consider all of the possibilities. Brainstorming with a friend will help this process and make it more fun. When you're finished reading, record your preferences in the Personal Portrait and Wishes Profile (see pages 27-29) for safekeeping.

QUESTION 1: WHAT ARE YOUR WISHES?

In this context, "wishes" are stipulations you make for how you want your celebration to be carried out. They can include legal or financial items provided for in your will, but should also include more simple requests if you have them. The focus here is on planning your memorial service, not distributing your estate, although both planning sessions can easily go hand-in-hand. When a wish costs money to execute, you will need to make sure you have allocated money from your estate to cover the costs.

Consider how your requests will affect others and how feasible they are to execute. In the end, whoever executes the actual event will consider the appropriateness of the request and make the ultimate decision. Perhaps Aunt Millie says she wants a line of limousines to carry everyone from the church to the reception. Her daughter might dismiss the request when planning the event, knowing that the gesture is much too ostentatious for her mother's crowd. She would want to save her mother from a dreadful mistake, knowing the wish would more likely anger people than leave the positive image she wanted. In a similar vein, you might stipulate that you want everyone to come in pajamas and think you have a very good reason, yet some people might not feel comfortable fulfilling your request.

If you have a wish you definitely want to be a part of your service, make sure you express that wish and explain its importance and then, if possible, speak directly to those ultimately responsible for its execution about it. If Aunt Millie wants the limousine escort because her most romantic memory was the night she rode in a limousine from the prom to a nightclub and fell in love with the man she eventually married, then explaining that during her memorial service would cast a completely different light on the gesture. People would ride in the limousines and take joy in one of her happiest memories.

Circumstance	Wish
Longtime scout leader or someone who likes pageantry	*Have an honor guard or other uniformed group standing at the entrance to the service*
High school music teacher, orchestra performer, or classical music enthusiast	*Make free tickets available to orchestra performances through the local high school to those who can't afford them*
Someone who wants alcohol served at a celebration without worrying about who will be driving home	*Arrange for a shuttle to pick up guests from the reception*

There are many aspects of a memorial service that you can personalize and arrange ahead of time. The following are some of the more common topics to consider when determining your wishes.

Place

Think about where you would like the celebration to happen, both the service and the reception. Remember not to judge your ideas, but rather think about all the possibilities and then narrow them down from there. Here are some questions to prompt your thinking:

- Is there a place of worship important to you?
- Where did you get married and/or hold your reception?
- Do you have a favorite park, hiking trail, or vacation spot?
- Where does your family gather for milestone celebrations?
- Is there a college alumni house, performance hall, or building that houses your favorite charity or nonprofit association?
- What are your favorite places to dance, party, or celebrate?
- Where do you go to think, renew yourself, or recharge?

After you make your list of places, the next step is to think about the feasibility of your ideas. For each place ask the following questions: Is it accessible? How will people get there? How many people can gather there? Will it require special logistical arrangements? Will it work in all kinds of weather or seasons? Also think about how your choices will affect those around you. Is there a stigma attached to the location that might make others uncomfortable? Is the choice out of financial reach for many of the attendees? Once you have narrowed your selections to the top two or three, make your final list. You do not need to limit your wishes to one idea, but rather provide a range of possible places and even plan for multiple celebrations.

Food and Drink

Food choices are important fingerprints of our heritage, part of the palette that paints our portrait; they can be the cornerstone of a community. There are many rituals around food based on traditions, and food also has the ability to create new traditions and create new bonds between friends and family. It is worthwhile to pay attention to what will be served at your reception and how it will portray who you are and where you come from. It is not about how much you spend, but more about the choices you make. Your friends and family are likely to think of you when they eat foods you have often shared with them. When you identify your wishes, try to include recipes—it will help build your legacy and give people another way to remember you.

If you invited your family and friends to a potluck what kind of spread would appear? Perhaps you are famous for your chocolate chip cookie recipe or widely recognized among loved ones as a peanut butter addict. Is there a favorite restaurant where you have frequently gathered, or a special place where you always celebrate important occasions? Here are some more questions to help you decide what food and drink should be served:

- What are your favorite foods? Is there anything from your childhood, heritage, or religion that is important to you?
- Is there someone in your life who cooked or baked something you really appreciated?
- Do you have any recipes you are known for?
- Are you a wine connoisseur? If anyone were to make a drink in your honor, what would it be?
- When gathering with friends or family what foods do you like to share with them?
- What is your favorite holiday and what special foods do you serve?

Music

Music is another important way to appeal to the senses during a memorial service. It can illustrate your personality, describing you in a way that words can't, and help create the right type of mood. When thinking about musical choices, consider the role you would like music to play in the service: Will it be a central part or simply an accent? Think beyond the traditional instruments and songs you hear associated with memorial services, and select music that reflects you and your preferences. Here are some questions you can ask yourself about the role music should play:

- What are your favorite songs from various eras, religious traditions, genres, or travels?
- Are you known for anything you have written or performed?
- What special songs do you remember from your childhood, a first or last dance, around the campfire, in school, or the military?
- What songs were played at your wedding?
- What songs speak to your heart?
- What songs will remind people of you the most?

QUESTION 2: HOW DO YOU WANT TO BE REMEMBERED?

My friend Pebble is a political activist who is wholeheartedly devoted to making the neighborhood, the country, and the world a better place. Her dining room table is forever covered with mailings asking people to help her causes. I am confident that she would like to be remembered as someone who made a difference in this world.

What have been the most important moments in your life? For many mothers, it is the act of giving birth and raising healthy, happy children. It can be as lofty as being remembered for inventions that saved lives or as simple as being a truly decent person. When you start planning early enough, you give yourself the opportunity to change those things that you might be afraid you will be remembered for. Let's say your expertise is downsizing companies and you are well known for laying off employees. You might be proud of how you help troubled companies survive, but you might also wish to be remembered for the less visible work you do in the local food pantry, helping those in need. Making people aware of the parts of your life you would like them to know about will help paint a more complete picture of you and the way you want to be remembered.

Perhaps you have no idea what people think about you. If you do not plan in advance, how will people remember you? There are many ways you can find out, but the best (and often easiest) way is to ask. Remember that there are many people from different periods in your life who will have different views of you and your accomplishments. You might also find that by asking people how they see you, it may help you recall forgotten experiences and accomplishments that you would have never otherwise considered.

What Will You Be Known For?

Depending upon when you start planning, you may discover that you still want to accomplish something you have yet to do. If you have already accomplished your goals, make sure your legacy is captured in a way that will have a presence at your memorial service. What do you consider as your most important life accomplishments? Do you wish to be remembered for your role in high school sports, or your more recent recreational exploits? If no one is left to remember that you were captain and a record-breaking quarterback for your high school football team, how will you make sure people know about that period in your life? Here are some questions that can help you determine how you most want to be remembered:

- What has been your greatest act of kindness, courage, ingenuity, or adventure?
- How will someone who knew you as a student, coworker, or neighbor remember you? Is it the same or different?
- What awards within your profession, associations, or hobbies have you received?
- Have you been a member of a club, association, or organization that is particularly meaningful to you? Is there a charity or cause that you believe in and have contributed to?
- What schools did you attend and would you like to be associated with them? Do you feel a debt of gratitude to a favorite professor or coach that you would like to recognize?
- What hobbies are you best known for?
- Do you like to travel? What have been your favorite trips?
- What profession will people recognize you for?

Living Legacies

There are other ways you can be remembered after the memorial service and reception are over. Living legacies, such as park benches or plaques, are becoming more and more common. Associating yourself with a certain time, place, or event—such as an annual athletic tournament, professional symposium, or a scholarship award—can also be a meaningful way to be remembered. If you have made a substantial contribution of your time, money, or expertise to an association, club, alma mater, religious group, or nonprofit organization and wish to be remembered in connection with them, then consider making plans ahead of time to ensure you receive the kind of recognition you would like. It is better to make stipulations for money you bequeath while you are healthy and able to personally negotiate the terms.

Stories

Oftentimes nothing paints a better picture of a person than the stories told about them. If you do not know the stories that best illustrate who you are, ask your close friends and relatives to share with you their favorite stories. Not only will you learn a little about how people perceive you, you will also be able to start thinking about the best speakers to relate these stories later on. When choosing stories or speakers, consider which stories portray you at your best or proudest moment, illustrate a life-changing experience, make you laugh (even if the event wasn't funny at the time), or convey your admiration for someone who influenced or inspired you. Think about who should tell these stories; different people might tell them in different ways. Also consider how you would want the stories presented; whether spoken aloud, in print, or recorded with audio or video. The delivery can change the way people interact with them.

Quotations and Poetry

Entertainers are famous for their memorable lines: Arnold Schwarzenhager for, "I'll be back;" James Bond's famous request for a martini, "Shaken not stirred;" or Clint Eastwood for, "Do you feel lucky? Do you?" In the everyday world, people sometimes adopt an often-repeated phrase that becomes a mantra, something indelibly characteristic. Is there a phrase, quotation, or expression that people associate with you? Maybe there is a poem, a section from a book or play, or a favorite religious passage that has always been important to you. Consider making these words part of your memorial service.

QUESTION 3: WHAT BEST SYMBOLIZES WHO YOU ARE?

What is most often missing from memorial services is the personalization that goes beyond choosing the scriptures, hymns, and what is said about the honoree. Even if you wish to have a traditional religious ceremony, there are many ways to bring additional comfort and joy to those attending your service. Sights, fragrances, flavors, sounds—each has the power to make us remember. A photograph is only one of countless things that will trigger memories of you. Think about what symbols are associated with you and find ways to incorporate them into your memorial service. You can be as creative or as traditional as you like—just remember to avoid overwhelming people with too many embellishments and only select those that are true to you.

Traditions

Few people go through life without some sense of tradition—even something as basic as democracy, standing up for what one believes in, or a truism such as "necessity is the mother of invention." Some people grow up with a strong sense of their cultural or religious heritage, intermingling old and contemporary traditions (for example, serving lasagna at Thanksgiving instead of turkey in a family with a strong Italian heritage). What traditions, current or ancient, do you value or identify with most? Are they expressed through religion, geography, your family name or crest, or a club you are associated with? There are a variety of rituals and practices from a range of cultures that can be brought forward into contemporary celebrations to create a very personal service.

Clothing

The visual unity of a group in uniform or similar dress can be a very powerful and striking symbol. If you decide you would like ushers, honor guards, speakers, or attendees to dress in a particular way, there are a few sources of inspiration that you can draw from. Think about what traditions, clubs, or organizations you have belonged to that might be visually represented at the service through a uniform or traditional costume. Do you identify with a style of dress from a particular historical period or cultural heritage, or are you known for wearing a particular style or item of clothing? Perhaps you have one beloved item that you are never without. Incorporating clothing into your service is an easy way to individualize the event.

Symbols

Symbols may or may not play a role in the planning of your memorial service, but thinking about their importance can help you develop an overall theme. Here are some questions you can ask yourself to determine what symbols, if any, are important to you:

- Is there a symbol that represents your name?
- Do you know your astrological symbol, and do you identify with it?
- Do you collect something that symbolizes who you are or what you like?
- Have you consistently had a particular kind of pet that people associate with you?
- Do you have a logo for your business, hobby, or organization?
- What is your favorite time of day? Are you an early-morning person, or do you love sunsets?

Flowers, Fauna, and Fragrance

If you want the ambiance of the service to include your favorite flowers, then explaining what those flowers mean to you is important. Is there a certain animal that you identify with, or one that is associated with your hobby or profession? Or maybe you are known for always carrying around peppermints; in that case, you may want to incorporate that particular taste in your service. What flowers, fauna, fragrance, or taste have meaning for you?

Color

Perhaps you are well known for a particular color, or conversely, detest one. What color or color themes reflect your preferences? Do they change and is that meaningful as well?

WRITE DOWN YOUR WISHES

After you have considered some of the options for personalizing your memorial service, you can start filling in your Personal Portrait and Wishes Profile. Consolidating all of your ideas into one document will not only help you organize your thoughts, it will also make communicating your wishes with your loved ones easier.

The Personal Portrait and Wishes Profile provides you with space to enter information for every category, but you should only fill in the sections that are important to you. Having too much information could easily overwhelm someone trying to execute your plan. Having a handwritten or computer printout of your profile avoids the problem of changing technologies. You will have a way to communicate clearly to others what is important to you in terms of likes, dislikes, and traditions.

While it is always a good idea to have a detailed written document stating your requests saved in a safe place for your executor, trusted relative, or friend, there are other ways to communicate your wishes. In addition to writing them out, you can also use a video camera or audio recorder to record stories and final wishes. When delivered as a first-person narrative, requests can become much more powerful and immediate.

Once you start thinking about planning for your memorial service, you may find yourself hearing or seeing things that you will want to include. Update your Personal Portrait and Wishes Profile regularly and keep it in a folder, computer file, or other easily accessible place. Include songs, poems, copies of well-written obituaries, recipes, thank-you notes, and anything else that appeals to or inspires you.

PERSONAL PORTRAIT & WISHES PROFILE

Name   *Date*

_____

For each category below, list the top one to three choices (more if it makes sense) and tell any important story or reason for your choices. You do not need to include wishes for each section. For those sections you do not complete, state why (such as, I don't care, or there aren't any symbols that are meaningful to me).

Traditions: What traditions do you wish to have represented in your service? Why?

_____
_____
_____
_____
_____

Music: What songs and instruments do you wish played, by whom, and why?

_____
_____
_____
_____
_____

Quotations, passages, and poetry: What do you wish read, printed, or used in some other way?

_____
_____
_____
_____
_____

Stories: What stories do you wish read, printed, or used in some other way?

_____
_____
_____
_____

Achievements: What achievements would you most like recognized in your service?

_____

_____

_____

_____

_____

Place: Where would you prefer to have your service and reception held?

_____

_____

_____

_____

_____

Food and drink: What food and drink do you wish served at your reception? Is there something special about where, by whom, or how you would like it served?

_____

_____

_____

_____

Flowers, fauna, and fragrance: What flowers, fruit, or other flora do you wish to have as part of the ceremony or reception? Is there any special way that you would like to incorporate them? Are there scents that reflect you? Do you have pets that you would like to have incorporated in the service?

_____

_____

_____

_____

Symbols: What symbols represent who you are? Is there any special way you would like to have them displayed?

_____

_____

_____

Color: What color or color scheme should dominate the service and/or reception and why?

_____

_____

_____

_____

_____

Clothing: What clothing theme, uniform, or style of dress would you like guests, ushers, or an honor guard to wear?

_____

_____

_____

_____

_____

Other gatherings and living legacies: In addition to or in place of a memorial service and reception, what other celebrations would you like held to remember you or your accomplishments?

_____

_____

_____

_____

Legacy plans: Should donations be made to a specific charity in your name in lieu of flowers?

_____

_____

_____

_____

Notes:

_____

_____

_____

_____

_____

Organize

3
Getting Started

If you are planning a service for someone other than yourself, it is best to look at the big picture before delving into the details. In the very early stages of planning, you have two top priorities: get the word out there and establish a basic layout for the service. This chapter will walk you through accomplishing both.

PLANNING THE SERVICE

There is no right or wrong order for a service, and no right or wrong inclusions or exclusions. For example, while you might find it difficult to imagine omitting music altogether, a service centered entirely on guided meditations can be a moving alternative. (If you think most guests will expect a traditional service and you are planning something different, it might be helpful to notify everyone in advance.) On the other hand, for many a traditional service (or a secular service based on a more traditional religious ceremony) will be the most comforting, both to plan and to experience.

However you choose to conduct the service, the kind of service you choose will have a great deal to do with its order and progression. Mapping out the service and determining the length of each component will prevent things from dragging on; very young and very elderly participants often find it difficult to remain comfortably seated for more than one hour. A service that lasts for thirty minutes is sufficient, while one that lasts longer than an hour is too long. The idea is to create a celebration that captures the highlights, not an exhaustive biography, of the honoree. The following section includes a plan for a traditional order of service. Use this framework as it is, or as a springboard for a more nontraditional service of your own creation.

The Traditional Elements

Prelude

Playing background music will help set the tone while people are gathering and waiting for a service to begin. Soft, quiet music will provide an atmosphere of reflection, while lively music will create a more uplifting mood. The prelude is a specific piece of music signaling that the service is about to begin and can be noted as such in the program. If the music or the performer has a connection to the honoree both can be listed in the program, otherwise you can just enter the heading "Prelude" or "Music."

Greeting

The greeting is your opportunity to welcome everyone. Whether secular or religious, these opening words will help put those attending at ease and let them know what to expect. You can also explain why you chose the particular tone and location of the service. If there are any special guests, you can recognize them in a way that pays homage to the honoree and their relationship to the guest. You can also take this opportunity to explain any symbols, songs, or other meaningful choices made for the service (although this can also take place later on). A greeting can be a poem, reading, prayer, or simply a call that guests sit closer toward the front. Whatever form the greeting takes, it is important to keep it brief.

Designate a greeter or someone else to stand by and preside over the service. This should be someone who is familiar with the order of the ceremony and will ensure each part begins at the correct time. This is also someone who can provide an explanation if a mistake is made or attend to a speaker who breaks into tears, runs on too long, or begins to say something in poor taste. Having a master of ceremonies who can walk over, put an arm around the speaker, and say, "Thank you very much," then walk the speaker to the side is an invaluable service both to the speaker and the audience.

Also called: call to worship

First Song or Hymn

The first song should be one that most guests will know and be able to sing easily. It should build a sense of community, bring people together to join in the celebration, and should provide a good introduction to the next piece in the service, both in tone and flow. Make sure the words do not contradict what the previous or following speakers say. It is also very important to have musical accompaniment to keep everyone singing together, even if it is in the form of experienced singers that help carry the rest of the group. Ask people to stand (if they are able) before and sit following the song. Whether you have chosen a hymn or a nontraditional song, include at least the title in the program; if desired, you can also include the words.

Words of Grace

A reading or prayer will quiet people and give them a moment to clear their thoughts and reflect upon why they have gathered. Depending upon the previous song, you can carry the same mood or shift it to prepare for the next section of the program.

Also called: opening prayer, invocation, meditation

Second Song or Hymn

If you would like to include more music, place an additional song here. In the traditional model, the musical progression moves from serene to jubilant.

Readings

The reading can be a poem, prose, or religious passage that reflects the taste, characteristics, or choice of the honoree. You can also use an interactive reading to include the attendees and develop a sense of community. Be careful to avoid anything controversial, as some people may find it uncomfortable speaking words they do not believe in or agree with. In the program, include the title or source of the reading and the name of the reader if it is someone other than the officiant.

Musical Interlude or Solo Performance

A traditional service often includes a musical interlude performed by someone other than the attendees, such as a choir, soloist, or musical ensemble. In a nontraditional service this is an opportunity to play something else meaningful to the honoree. If there are no performers, you can play a recording of the piece. Many venues have good sound systems, but an iPod or MP3 player will also work.

Third Song or Hymn

Depending on the target length of the service and how much music you wish to include, you may decide to incorporate a third song or hymn. If you plan a service with a lot of music, remember that singing fewer verses of more songs will make the service more interesting and move along at a faster pace.

Eulogies and Speeches

For many people the eulogy is the most meaningful and important part of the memorial service. For this reason, it is important to make sure this portion of the service is well prepared. When creating the program, determine the order of the speakers by relevance to the honoree or to ensure that the most celebratory speech is the last one. In the program, be sure to include a title for each speech (perhaps based on theme or time period in the honoree's life, or perhaps a quote from the actual speech) as well as relevant information about the speaker's relationship to the honoree.

Also called: reflections, in memoriam, memories, words of remembrance, homily

Closing Song or Hymn

The parting song or hymn will create the mood people will carry to the reception. Traditionally it should create an air of jubilation, leaving people ready for lively conversation and reminiscing at the reception.

Parting Words

Before the final pronouncement, remind people that the family has invited them to a reception. (If the reception is not held at the same location as the service, consider including an insert in the program with directions and a small map.) In your closing remarks, thank everyone for coming and joining the celebration. You can also express your appreciation to anyone who contributed to the service but was not introduced or otherwise acknowledged earlier. Your words should be uplifting and leave guests with a sense of closure and peace.

Also called: benediction

Postlude

From the New Orleans jazz classic "When the Saints Go Marching In" to a religious recessional hymn, this musical selection should be a celebration symbolizing the send-off of the honoree. The music can be performed in the background, foreground, or as a group processional.

Even if the service is traditional in every other way, consider having a little fun with this final musical piece. If the honoree was a Beatles fanatic, concluding the service with an instrumental rendition of one of the band's classics would make a memorable finish. The postlude sets the mood that guests carry with them to the reception. Unless the honoree's final wishes instruct otherwise, the music that plays as people leave the service should be uplifting and jubilant.

LAYING OUT THE SERVICE

Now that you are familiar with the components of a traditional memorial service, you can begin picking and choosing which elements you wish to include in your own service. Use the chart on the next page to compile information for the program. As a rule, if the service includes any poems, songs, prayers, or scripture passages the titles of those works should appear in the program.

Title	Titles of Works and Participants	Time (in minutes)
Prelude	Title: Performer:	
Greeting	Speaker:	
First Song/Hymn (optional)	Title of Work: Performer:	
Words of Grace	Speaker:	
Second Song/Hymn (optional)	Title of Work: Performer:	
Reading(s)	Title of Work: Reader: Title of Work: Reader: Title of Work: Reader:	
Musical Interlude	Title of Work: Performer:	
Third Song/Hymn (optional)	Title of Work: Performer:	
Eulogies/Speeches	Speaker: Speaker: Speaker: Speaker:	
Closing Song/Hymn (optional)	Title of Work: Performer:	
Parting Words	Speaker:	
Postlude	Title of Work: Performer:	

PROGRAM BASICS

Once you have organized the service you will have the information you need to design the program. Using a computer desktop publishing program, you can produce an inexpensive yet elegant black-and-white program. Most programs are based on standard paper sizes, which can then be folded, stapled, or stitched. While there are many options, the typical program is simply a folded 8.5 x 11 sheet of paper. If you want a simpler, inexpensive program, you can also print on a half sheet and include only essential information.

If you need to include words to songs or readings, you may need a larger sheet size, which will also give ample room to add a photo of the honoree on the front, some quotations sprinkled throughout, and perhaps a short biography, poem, or song on the back. If you would like to include all of the service elements, such as verses and song lyrics, add a half- or full-sheet insert. If you know there will be older people attending, make sure the print size is large enough for easy reading.

Adding a photograph will instantly make the program more personal. Select a picture that is flattering both because of its quality and because it captures the honoree's essence: a cheerful, thoughtful, or youthful pose, or perhaps one of the honoree doing something he or she loved. If you can't print the photo yourself, have them printed separately and insert them into the programs. If you are going to add clip art to dress up your program, be sure to only use high-quality graphics. (The clip art collection from Dover Publications will give you a professional selection.)

For a simple service, you can skip printing individual programs and create one or two large posters; just make sure they are readable from a distance and placed where everyone can see them. You can also use a projector and presentation software to guide people through the service with slides or images.

Creating a Keepsake

A program can become an important memento in and of itself. If you have the time, inclination, and funds you can create one that people will want to keep. In the same way that a menu reflects the quality and atmosphere of a restaurant, the program will reflect the memorial service. Professional typesetting and design, color, and quality paper stock will transform a traditional program into something more enduring and impressive.

If you have among your friends a graphic designer, then you may have the opportunity to create a visually stunning and memorable program. I find many people keep the program from a service in memory of those they love, but they are more likely to appreciate and find comfort in it if the program includes memories from the service, such as the words to readings, songs, and quotations.

One of the most memorable programs I have in my collection is from the service for my cousin. The program is a standard folded 8.5 x 11 sheet. Because of the amount of content, there is a second folded sheet inside, making the program eight pages. The cover includes a picture of my cousin and the overall look is artistic but simple, using ivory, linen-finish paper stock and brown ink. Words to poems and songs are included, but what makes it truly special is a graphic display of the family tree along with some family history included in the center spread. As an added touch, attendees were also given a small stapled booklet, in the same paper stock and ink color as the program, which featured thoughtfully selected black-and-white photographs of the honoree through the years. The booklet was tucked into a brown envelope. Because it is slightly larger than a CD or DVD envelope, photos, videos, recordings, or scanned guestbook pages from the service or reception could later be tucked into the envelope along with the booklet.

An additional stapled booklet can hold many different kinds of memories. In addition to the complete program, you can also include eulogies, readings and song verses, a family tree, and more photos than a traditional program. Whatever the format, the outcome will be a memorable keepsake, and one that has the advantage of avoiding ever-changing technology. You cannot be sure the DVD format of the keepsake you create will be compatible with the equipment in generations to come. (However, having video and photos captured digitally can be very rewarding and historically significant for a family and should not be overlooked.)

If tackling a book-like program seems too overwhelming, there are some other very simple printed pieces you can create as mementos: postcards or bookmarks are two very easy examples. There are many full-color printing companies that specialize in high-quality, low-cost postcard production, and guarantee fast printing times. A standard-size postcard will hold a great deal of information: a picture, a brief biography, a favorite passage, song, or quotation. If the honoree has a special symbol or token, consider attaching a tassel or charm.

One of my favorite mementos from a service I attended is a bookmark. It is brightly colored and laminated, obviously something to keep. A bookmark is something people can use to mark a special passage that will bring back memories every time they turn to it. In addition to a picture of the honoree, consider including a favorite passage, prayer, quotation, or even a treasured family recipe.

While all of the examples so far have been printed on paper stock, there are many other alternatives to traditional programs—you don't even have to print on paper. If the honoree is a person who everyone knew from the local coffee shop, then hand out a coffee mug with the program printed on it, or maybe a picture, lifespan dates, and a favorite saying. For someone who eschewed formality, printing the service's order, a photograph, and a quotation on a T-shirt might be fitting. These examples are all creative yet appropriate ways to mark the occasion of a memorial service. Just remember when you start getting creative that the program has a practical purpose as well. You will need to make sure people can still use the program to lead them through the service.

Let your imagination play with the different symbols, flowers, colors, hobbies, and professional artifacts while you think about all of the different ways you can give people something to take home with them in remembrance of the honoree. Here are a few more ways to have fun creating memorable keepsakes:

- For an honoree who loved shoes, attach the program or a small booklet to a miniature craft shoe with a ribbon.
- Give everyone a colored, votive candle. Wrap it in a colorful cotton or silk print, tie with a ribbon, and attach a small card with a quotation or small picture.

- For someone who loved the sea, place a seashell in a small silk bag and tie the bag closed with a ribbon in the honoree's favorite color.
- For a gardener, make small sachets filled with sprigs of lavender or pine needles.
- If the honoree was a roofer, attach the program to a slate tile or shingle.

NOTICES

No matter how thorough you are about putting a death notice in the relevant newspapers, there is no guarantee that everyone will see it. And while bad news travels fast, nothing is worse than finding out that a friend has died long after the memorial service has already taken place.

Announcement Card

According to the *Ladies Handbook and Household Assistant,* published in 1886, publishing a notice in the newspaper will suffice for distant friends and relatives, "but near and dear friends of the deceased should be informed by note written on mourning paper . . . unless the distance it too great, [they] should be sent by private messenger." How times have changed. Now a newspaper notice is unlikely to reach all of an honoree's friends and acquaintances, even when published in multiple newspapers spanning the states and countries where an honoree lived. In fact, circumstances have almost come full circle—it might now be more expedient to publish a notice locally and send notices to those who live a distance from the honoree.

In the past you may have sent wedding, birth, or graduation notices. In certain circumstances, a mailed notice announcing the death of the honoree and the memorial service details might be the best way to quickly inform those who will want to attend. Your extra effort will be gratefully appreciated. Postcards work well and are simple and efficient, while an invitation-size card and envelope, on the other hand, might be more elegant and personal.

For an honoree with an up-to-date address book or annual Christmas card list, eliminate all local and business addresses, leaving a core mailing list. The notice can be brief or long, depending on how much information you include. If you send them immediately, you might not yet have details about the time and place for the memorial service. If you plan to hold the service sometime in the future rather than immediately, your notice will be even more appreciated. If you can afford it, for a nominal amount beyond the cost of postage, you can upload your address list, picture, and text to an online service and have your postcard sent out for you (see Resources).

Newspaper Notice

Newspaper notices have also been evolving. No longer are they a simple acknowledgement of who, what, when, and where. It is rare that you see a memorial service notice published without an obituary. The obituary is now often a celebration and acknowledgment of an honoree's accomplishments and attributes.

It is important to recognize the changing role of the obituary. Obituaries of the past were stilted, somber, and except for the famous, were generally quite short. Reading the obituary of an "ordinary" person would have had no place in a celebratory memorial service. Today, obituaries are more often written in the tradition of a press release featuring successes, accomplishments, and triumphs—capturing the best of every individual. A well-written biographical obituary read at a memorial service can be the cornerstone eulogy, set an uplifting tone, and be included on the program or as part of the memorabilia.

When publishing an obituary with a memorial service notice, consider writing it like a press release. What is newsworthy? What do you want future generations to know and remember about this person? Obituaries are a snapshot of accomplishments and an opportunity to document a person's life for posterity. There are gifted people who can turn a litany of accomplishments into a memorable, historical, newsworthy newspaper article. If necessary, hire or ask someone who has good writing skills to help.

Blogs and personal websites are giving everyone a chance to write obituaries their own way. Regardless of all this freedom, it is important to write an obituary that will paint the honoree in the best light, while thinking about the short- and long-term importance of the notice.

Memorial Service Notice

In addition to the obituary you will also want to publish information about the memorial service in the relevant newspapers, if it is open to the public. In the notice, specify any special instructions for those attending. You might want people to bring something, wear a specific article of clothing or color, or be prepared to participate in the service in some way. If you've created a website in memory of the honoree with information about the upcoming service, include the web address in your newspaper notice. However, remember to be inclusive for those who still prefer a newspaper over the Internet. If you allow the public to contribute to the website, make sure you can screen (and potentially reject) what is posted.

While few death notices are just about inviting people to the memorial service, there are hurried occasions where you will want to use a notice in lieu of a full obituary. If you know that the service will not be held immediately after the honoree's death, you might choose to send personal invitations instead.

THE GUESTBOOK

Even if you are not anticipating a large crowd, have more than one guestbook available for signing during the memorial service. Even a small number of participants can create a bottleneck at the service's entrance, especially if people are doing more than just signing in. (You can suggest that people sign the book at the reception, though you might miss people who attended only the service.)

There are many ways for you to explore alternatives to a traditional guestbook. One of the easiest ways is to personalize a standard book by pasting photographs onto pages and incorporating stamps, stickers, illustrations, quotations, or symbols. Or, move away from the traditional book format and create a large poster of the honoree that people can sign. Have two or more posters if you are expecting a large crowd and provide a variety of colors, widths, and types of markers for people to choose from. You can also have a laptop set up at the reception for people to enter their favorite story, saying, or sentiments. (Waiting until the reception will give people more time to think about what to say.) While there are programs that allow people to set up online memorials, when people act anonymously they are more likely to say hurtful things. A more controlled environment will encourage people to exercise better judgment. There are computers and programs that allow people to use a writing tablet rather than a keyboard if you are concerned about whether attendees are computer literate.

A memory box is another alternative to a guestbook, and one that will result in more personal responses. People can bring a picture with a note on the back, a typed or handwritten page with a story, or another expression to deposit in the box. Of course, you can use a traditional guestbook in addition to the memory box. You will want to include a brief statement in the memorial service notice to let people know they are welcome to contribute to a memory box, as well as a brief explanation of what you are asking for.

Another way to gather personal responses is to hand out a questionnaire with the program and encourage guests to fill them out and drop them off as they leave. Writing down memories will give people something to do while they are waiting for the service to begin. Questions can include: How did you and the honoree first meet? Tell the funniest story you know that involves the honoree. What is your fondest memory of the honoree? Where did you see the honoree most often? What was the most unlikely place you ever ran into him/her? What saying do you remember the honoree for best? What words best describe the honoree?

The guestbook can also be part of the venue itself. For example, if the service is held on the family ranch or a lake house, pick a wall, door, or other surface and have attendees sign their names and write their messages in chalk, markers, or paint. If the writing can only be temporary, make sure you

FIVE TIPS FOR A WELL-PLANNED SERVICE

· Do sing songs and read passages that positively reflect the honoree and hold meaning for those attending. Controversial readings and music have no place at a memorial service.

· Do ask all speakers to share their talks beforehand to screen for redundant and inappropriate material. If two speakers plan to read the same poem or passage, encourage them to perform the piece as a duet.

· Do ensure the service lasts only one hour by timing each component beforehand.

· Do provide guests with a program that shows them the layout of the service.

· Do create a DVD or photo journal to share with family and friends who were unable to attend the service.

get a good photograph of the inscriptions and the inscribers. To make marker and chalk signatures permanent, preserve the wall with a lacquer coating. For generations to come it will be a unique place of remembrance.

WHEN PEOPLE ASK TO HELP

One of the kindest preparations you can make is being ready to respond to those who ask to help. For many it is an expression of their respect or love and a way of showing support for those closest to the honoree.

Not all people have the same skills, and not everyone will be able to help in the same way. A good way to navigate offers of help, for all involved, is to have a checklist of tasks. Using a checklist not only allows you to keep track of what tasks are being performed and by whom, but also gives those offering help a ready-made list of options to choose from. For some, this list may provide inspiration for a different type of contribution, perhaps something more personal or relevant to them. If someone offers to do something more specific, then it is easy enough to add it to the list.

Here is an example of a planning checklist. Remember, it is important to make sure people are capable and committed to completing their tasks and to follow up with them.

PLANNING CHECKLIST

Task	Name	Date due
Notices • Write an obituary of the honoree in press-release style • Address/stamp envelopes for invitations or other notifications using the honoree's address book or holiday list		
Transportation • Drive people to and from the airport, hotel, or memorial service • Pick up floral arrangements after the service and take them to the reception • Pick up sentimental/valuable objects used in the memorial service/reception and return them safely to the owner		
Ceremony • Serve as a greeter or usher • Give a eulogy • Create a display of photographs and/or sentimental objects		
Food • Bring a dish for the reception		
Other Tasks • Design and/or make copies of the program • Supply a guestbook for the service		

Creativity

4

Personalizing Your Celebration

Whether you are aiming for simple or elaborate, creating the right atmosphere takes planning. With a little imagination and forethought, you will discover countless ways to embellish a memorial service. Here are a few examples of people who chose to celebrate their way.

MORE THAN A SIMPLE SERVICE

When a high-profile person dies and the number of those who wish to attend the memorial service exceeds what a simple ceremony can accommodate, a different kind of event might be in order. This was the case for a doctor known by many as the "Father of American Dermatology." Not only was he a pioneer in his field, he was also a teacher who had influenced students and colleagues worldwide.

Because this man was such a public figure, his family, who had already held a private funeral service for him, gave their blessing to his teaching hospital to plan a series of events to remember him. The first was a memorial service to celebrate his role as a family man, beloved teacher, and noted Harvard graduate. The second was a symposium to recognize his importance to the worldwide medical community and to raise money for a scholarship fund in his name. He died in August, and the memorial service and symposium were to be held in October. My company was called upon to coordinate the events, working as a team with the hospital and a committee of his colleagues.

To plan the service, I visited the widow and spoke with the family. I learned that the doctor held his Irish heritage close to his heart, loved chocolate and orchids, and had a deep appreciation for classical music. I also learned that Katherine Hepburn had been a patient of his. On one occasion, he asked a colleague to stop by Ms. Hepburn's hospital room to examine her and offer a second opinion. The next time he saw Hepburn, she purportedly scolded him, "Why did you send that intern to examine me?" She obviously did not know that so-called "intern" was a renowned international specialist in dermatology. With a story as delightful as this one, it became important not only to find a doctor who could relate the story at the service, but also to make sure that doctor's recollection was the same as the family's.

Because the doctor's family shared their memories with me, I was able to add simple touches to the service that made it more meaningful, not only to those attending but also to those participating: for the son who helped find a traditional Irish Uilleann pipe-player, for the widow who noticed the chocolate Hershey's Kisses sprinkled on the tabletops at the reception, for the friend who appreciated the significance of the orchids, for the longtime colleague who told the Katherine Hepburn story, and for those who paused and listened to the string quartet playing classical music during the symposium. I also suggested that the ushers—all young physicians from his hospital—all wear their white hospital coats, the way they appeared every day at work. Having their presence as his honor guard was a striking, immediate reminder that the honoree's life work would carry on. Everyone was taken by the homage these doctors paid, ushering the service in their uniforms, stethoscopes around their necks.

Other small touches included a tent in Harvard Yard decorated with pumpkins, cornstalks, and bittersweet so people who had traveled from afar could experience the festivity of a New England October. Other embellishments were more intimate. As a physician, his trade required the daily use of some specialized instruments, such as the loupe dermatologists use to examine patients. These medical tools were displayed on a black velvet cloth at the reception, allowing people to handle the instruments and reflect on him using them. Alongside the instruments was the remarkable notebook the doctor always carried, bursting with papers and held together with a rubber band. Everyone familiar with him chuckled as they passed it. There were also documents from his personal files propped on small, elegant brass wire easels against a black velvet backdrop, which turned a chaotic box of clutter into an accessible, distinguished display.

The service, held at Memorial Church in Harvard Yard, included the haunting, moving sounds of Uilleann pipes playing first distantly in the vestibule of the church, then close as guests filed out past the pipes player, and then distant again as the sounds accompanied their procession to the president's house for the reception. The symposium was an opportunity for the doctor's students and colleagues from around the world to gather and discuss how he had enriched their knowledge of dermatology. Interwoven with the lectures were touches of remembrance, including the string quartet playing Bach's concerto "Sheep May Safely Graze" in one of the large lecture halls. The music, among other thoughtful details, transformed this gathering into something more than just a scientific symposium.

A MEMORIAL WEEKEND

When my friend Sarah died, her family and close friends planned two days of activities to honor her. In much the same way that arrangements for a destination wedding are made, the family reserved hotel space and created a schedule of events for a weekend-long gathering that included a morning walk, a day spent exploring nearby coastal sites, and the informal launch of the foundation Sarah dreamed of starting—a retreat center for cancer patients. People gathered for dinner, told stories, remembered Sarah fondly, and took comfort in each other's company.

The final event was the scattering of Sarah's ashes into the Atlantic. Because of laws requiring that ashes be scattered at least three miles from the shoreline, only her immediate family planned to accompany Sarah's ashes out to sea. The rest of us gathered on the lawn sloping down to the dock next to the boathouse, waiting with a case of chilled Veuve Cliquot, Sarah's favorite champagne. We watched the boat head out to sea, Sarah's brother at the wheel. When we got a call from the boat announcing that Sarah's ashes were being scattered, the chilled Veuve Cliquot was brought out, and a twenty-first century pyrotechnic cannonade of fireworks was set off in tribute. The popping champagne corks and fireworks provided an unforgettable chorus of send-off salutes for Sarah.

JAZZ PARADE

Inspiration can come from the most unlikely places. A few years ago I received an invitation to the fiftieth birthday celebration for my good friend and bon vivant, Ron. I never suspected that the occasion would spark such a brilliant idea for a memorial service.

Ron is socially outgoing, both artistic and visionary, and has a wonderful sense of occasion. He is a landscape architect who works with city planners around the world, helping them establish a sense of identity within their communities. Public art is one of his passions. He is also known for entertaining in grand style. A month before his party, he sent out invitations with the date, time, and meeting location as well as a couple of extra instructions: Dress in something exclusively black, white, or some combination of both and wear comfortable walking shoes.

It was a warm, clear evening in early June. There were about fifty revelers, a striking group all clothed in black and white. We gathered at one of Ron's clubs, an elegant, traditional building on Beacon Hill. Mint juleps and hors d'oeuvres were served in the garden and we toasted our host. Then we began our jubilant march, following Ron with his twinkling blue eyes and tall frame in a white linen suit, on a well-mapped course of his favorite vistas. A New Orleans-style jazz band accompanied us on our journey. At each stop the musicians played a flourish as we saluted the particular work of public art or vista of landscaped beauty and listened to their joyful strains. At one point in the journey we released balloons inscribed with handwritten birthday wishes. Along our processional route, festive refreshments were served at the Boston Public Library, where Ron had an exhibit of his work on display. We capped off the evening with a lovely dinner at the Tavern Club, a hidden jewel of Boston's artistic and theatrical tradition.

It occurred to me later that a reenactment of the jazz procession, in turn an adaptation of the New Orleans jazz funeral tradition, might be the perfect send-off for someone. It creates a joyous gathering of friends for those who love music or walking or want to share a personal view of their world. A procession offers many opportunities for customization—the music doesn't have to be jazz; it could be anything.

UPLIFTING SENTIMENTS

One of the most moving moments during the remembrance weekend for Sarah was when the champagne corks popped and the fireworks launched. The meaning behind these joyous symbols, carrying their message of good wishes into the sky, provided a wonderful emotional release. Here are a few more ways you can replicate this feeling of sending off your best wishes.

White Doves

The image of twenty snow-white doves flying heavenward, circling above, and then journeying back to their home loft is a breathtaking sight. In the Christian tradition, doves represent the soul, angels, and the Holy Spirit. At a memorial service, they are powerful witnesses of the spirit's passage to Heaven.

In a standard dove release at least twelve trained white doves are set free from a white wicker basket. When the doves are released they fly around in the sky orienting themselves and then, once they have their bearings, head straight home.

Today, a dove release is something that can be privately arranged through the White Dove Release Directory of America (see Resources). This is a service that is available on a complimentary basis for firefighters, peacekeepers, or police killed in the line of duty. Conditions for a successful dove release include having a loft within fifty miles of the site of the memorial service, daylight, and reasonable weather.

Butterflies

A butterfly release is striking and symbolically stirring. It is also less expensive than you might think. There are many services that will humanely ship butterflies for release, but before you order check for any local restrictions and observe the conditions necessary for a successful release. The release should take place when the temperature is above sixty degrees in fair weather with no rain (in order to keep the butterflies safe and dry), and must take place at least an hour and a half before sunset (see Resources).

Bubbles

At memorial services that include children (or children at heart), providing soap liquid and bubble wands is an easy way to add a hint of playfulness. Blowing bubbles gives people a way to participate at the end of the service, plus they are beautiful to watch. Giving away soap bubbles as memorial favors to be taken to children who did not attend can also be an effective way to remember the honoree after the service.

Balloons

A balloon release is another expression of reaching out and up. Unlike the other releases, which are strictly visual, balloons give participants the opportunity to send messages into the sky. Selecting balloons in a color that is representative of the honoree can make the release even more meaningful. Consider giving guests a permanent marker to write a message or favorite quote, their name, a place, or a song title or verse. Since balloon releases can potentially be harmful to the environment, it is important to select and release balloons correctly. There are also professionals who help with releases. If you choose to do it yourself, follow these earth-friendly guidelines:

- Make sure the balloons are latex, which is a natural biodegradable substance. Never use plastic or Mylar.
- Less is better than more. As few as ten balloons can be symbolic and will not overwhelm the environment.
- Do not release anything else, such as a string, with the balloon.

Consider a dove or butterfly release in places where balloons are outlawed, or if the service is held near an aquatic habitat.

UNIFORMS AND DISTINCTIVE CLOTHING

When we all gathered for Ron's birthday parade dressed in black and white, we immediately became a group with something in common. Everyone cleared a path as we marched (which may also have had something to do with our jubilant noisemaking). But creating the illusion of a group in uniform was an empowering gesture.

Uniforms add a sense of pageantry to a service. There is something very stirring about people in uniform, standing at attention, hands clasped behind them or straight at their sides—even if it is only the local Boy Scout troop. If the honoree is closely associated with a uniformed group, such as a Scout troop, military attachés, or sports team, ask if the group will participate in the service. If the honoree has no affiliation to a group in any kind of uniform, there are a variety of ways to incorporate items of clothing or badges that will help create the same type of solidarity. Here are three primary ways to use uniforms:

· An honor guard serving at either the entranceway or front of the service
· Ushers or escorts
· A symbolic item of clothing given to everyone who attends the service

For a museum docent or hospital volunteer, ask colleagues to wear their identification badges; for a chef, ask colleagues to wear their toques. For a hockey player, have teammates suit up and form an archway with their sticks for guests to pass under as they enter the service. If the honoree loved the West, request that every guest wear cowboy boots, hats, and kerchiefs (or hand out bandannas to everyone at the reception). Religious traditions, if appropriate, also offer a wealth of symbols. Tibetan prayer shawls, Jewish yarmulkes, Catholic rosaries—any of these items could make a sentimental keepsake for those who attend the service.

THE CHALLENGE

These examples show the possibilities for creating a service that is relevant yet still reverent. Whether you desire a celebratory service or one that is more somber and reflective, your choices will set the tone.

Some of these events require extensive planning, others a moderate amount. But all of them require someone paying attention to the details and overseeing the orchestration. When planning a memorial service for someone other than yourself, spend some time reflecting on what was important to the honoree. What were their passions, their favorite things, their proudest moments? The answers to these questions will guide you to what type of memorial service the honoree would have wanted, and will likely inspire you with ways of making the service more personal and meaningful.

5
Finding the Right Place

Location. Location. Location.

Consider what type of ambience you want for the service and then choose your venue accordingly. A service in a traditional Christian church feels completely different from a jazz procession through a city street; a reception in a banquet hall feels different from one in a state park. Like weddings, there are a multitude of venues available and you will certainly be able to find one that suits your needs. But also just like weddings, memorial celebrations can either be outrageously extravagant, modest, or somewhere in between. When it comes time to choose a venue for the memorial service and reception, the first step is to consult the wishes of the honoree. If no instructions were left behind, and perhaps even no funding put aside for a service, there are still a number of ways to pay tribute.

Talk with relatives or friends, agree on an appropriate budget, and then proceed from there. While it's best to hold the memorial service within a reasonable time period (at least within one year), you do not have to rush into making an immediate decision. Take the time to do it right.

LESS EXPENSIVE VENUES
An economical memorial service does not have to look cheap. Unlike many

other events, a memorial service can be held during any season, on any day of the week, and at any time of day. This means that venues may not always be in high demand. You may not need a Friday night or Saturday afternoon, which tend to be the most expensive times to rent a space.

If the venue you are considering charges a rental fee, ask if they will consider a reduction or exception because of the nature of the event. In the same way, if the honoree was a member of a club or organization, ask to use their facilities. (Emphasize your willingness to rent the space during off-peak hours, if you can do so). Many cities and towns have free community spaces, such as parks, pavilions, libraries, or municipal buildings. Your local chamber of commerce can tell you about free venues in your area.

Another resource for venues is your community's events calendar; most are now online or in the local newspaper. Browse the last few months of listings to give you an idea of what is available. You can also ask the local caterers where they have worked events in the past. Whatever venue you choose, be sure to ask whether a permit is required for a public gathering, whether food and beverages are allowed, and if tables and chairs are included. (Chair and table rentals can be expensive, so look for connections within your community. You may be able to borrow them from a local school or other organization, or even ask attendees to bring their own lawn chairs for an outside event.)

The more you can relate a free or low-cost venue to the interests or attributes of the honoree, the more meaningful it will be. For example, a tailgate party for a football enthusiast, a barbeque for the grill master, afternoon tea in a garden for the member of the bridge group, a school cafeteria potluck for a teacher, or a waterfront picnic for the outdoor enthusiast are all ways to celebrate the individuality of the honoree without great expense. Also consider the possibility of using a relative or friend's personal residence to hold a memorial service. For slightly more money you can rent space in a museum, which could be especially meaningful if the honoree had a personal connection there. If you can afford to spend a little money, renting space in an orchard, winery, or yacht club are also options. For a small group, a dinner cruise might work perfectly.

Food is another way to control the cost of a memorial service. It does not have to be elaborate, but it is expected, and it can be one of the greatest expenses. While it might be tempting to serve traditional finger food, such as platters of cheese, vegetables, dips, and crackers, you can easily enrich the offerings by asking for help. Sharing food is an act that brings communities together, and oftentimes people will happily prepare a dish to share with others. This can be especially meaningful if the honoree was known for a certain traditional family recipe or cuisine. Whatever it is, the food that people bring will only further honor the memory of the honoree.

Food choices can also be tied to the time of day you choose to have the memorial service. There may be a time of day that best suits your budget. For example, a full dinner or luncheon will not be expected following a service at 10 a.m. or 2 p.m. People will only expect modest fare, making this a perfect time to have punch, tea, coffee, and a selection of cookies or simple hors d'oeuvres.

Dressing up the venue is another easy way to turn inexpensive into elegant. Renting colorful table linens (make sure they reach the floor and cover the table legs) with coordinating seat covers can enrich even the most industrial environment. You can also rent battery-powered table lamps to soften the atmosphere.

MORE EXTRAVAGANT VENUES

If you have the funds and wish to do something extravagant, there are infinite options. An easy way to explore ideas is to draw on the tourism and wedding industries. While a destination wedding *creates* memories, the destination memorial service should *reflect* on memories. For a couple whose honeymoon, family vacations, and fiftieth wedding anniversary were celebrated on Waikiki Beach, Honolulu, hosting a destination memorial service there would be appropriate. Honoring the family roots by holding a gathering in a Scottish castle or staying at a private resort in the Bahamas in memory of a special family vacation are other examples of meaningful destination memorial services. You could also go someplace the honoree never went to but always dreamed of visiting.

Once everyone has gathered you can make the ceremony as formal or informal as you wish, as the act of traveling and gathering in a meaningful place is in itself a big part of remembrance. (If nothing else, everyone should be prepared to do one unifying gesture, such as giving a toast). More than just a place, you will want to plan activities for guests so there are meaningful interactions and plenty of time to reflect and celebrate. Plan the event far enough in advance to allow people to arrange their schedules. You should include an RSVP request with the invitation, even though people are not accustomed to responding for a memorial service. In fact, anytime an event includes a sit-down dinner or other per-person fee, you are justified in requesting to know whether someone plans to attend or not.

Destination Newport

Hypothetically, let's say I was asked to plan a destination memorial celebration with a guest list of approximately thirty people. I'm informed that the honoree had close ties to Newport, Rhode Island. He was a former naval officer, an alumnus of Portsmouth Priory, loved jazz, and a skilled tennis player.

In this case, I'd plan far enough in advance to hold the celebration on a weekend in July. Newport is beautiful in the summer months. The memorial service could be held at Portsmouth Priory, which has a gorgeous seaside setting, and all the guests could stay together at a nearby inn.

Friends and family could fly into either Providence or Newport on Friday afternoon, where they would be met by a spiffy replica of a trackless trolley and whisked to their accommodations. In their rooms guests would find a bag with bottled water, an assortment of the honoree's favorite candies, brochures on local attractions, and a program with the weekend's itinerary. The first meal would be an informal reception on Friday night, welcoming everyone with a selection of great food and wine. A jazz quartet, performing some of the honoree's favorite tunes, would play softly throughout the evening.

A buffet-style, continental breakfast would be available early Saturday morning, giving guests adequate time for a walk or jog on the beach. I might also arrange for a naturalist to lead a beach walk for those who want to learn about the abundant shore birds of the area. At 10 a.m., the memorial service would be held in the Priory's chapel. Designed by Italian-American visionary

Paolo Soleri, this intimate chapel is a serene, beautiful place, ideal for reflection and prayer.

At the memorial service family and friends would pay tribute to the honoree with a short traditional service. In addition, the honoree's widow would announce an endowment fund, a living legacy, created in the honoree's name for his alma mater. She would also draw the connection of how the mission of the school embodied her late husband's spirit, the Benedictine education is grounded in the intellectual tradition of Ancient Greece and Rome, and balanced by a focus on spirituality, athletics, the arts, and fun.

Shortly following the memorial service, guests could head over to the Newport grass tennis courts for a tournament. A catered New England clambake would be served to those watching, finished with their matches, or awaiting their turn to play.

In the evening, guests would be taken for a ride on the dinner train from Newport to Portsmouth, and then given a tour of the school where the endowment would be established. The chair of the English department could give a talk on how the generous donation will benefit his department. Back at the inn, there would be a screening of the honoree's favorite film, Casablanca, for those wanting to continue the evening's events.

Sunday, after a buffet breakfast, everyone would ride the trackless trolley to Newport's waterfront and board a chartered wooden schooner. After touring the harbor and nearby coastline, they would land for a catered lunch on the beach. The menu would include a special punch (rum optional!), a well-known concoction of the honoree. With professional musicians to accompany them, everyone would sing songs and exchange fond memories. The singing might even continue on board as the cruise returns everyone to port.

As the afternoon winds down, people would either be escorted to their departure airport or left to explore on their own and relax. Tea sandwiches and other light snacks would be available as guests say their good-byes and depart.

As you can see, the possibilities for a meaningful, high-end celebration are vast. You just need to be willing to narrow in on the details and put the arrangements in place.

THE MOST LIKELY VENUE

If the honoree was a member of a particular house of worship or an active member of a religious community, then holding a memorial service in that religious setting may be the most appropriate act of remembrance. However, before you make a final decision, you should ensure that the location will accommodate all of your needs, have enough space for your guests, and have a suitable reception area. Also, if a champagne toast is an important part of your celebration and alcohol is not allowed, or if you need to prepare or keep food warm or cold, then you will need to hold the reception elsewhere.

Flexibility is also important in terms of the guests themselves, as there is no way to anticipate the actual number of attendees. What do you do when an unexpectedly large number of people show up? You may simply need to acknowledge the overwhelming response and ask people to forgive the lack of accommodations. Everyone will. A memorial service is not like a wedding or other event in which you are asking for presents or money. If you are anticipating unpredictable numbers, having a larger venue available as a backup can save the day. (For example, some houses of worship have multiple venues on their premises).

If the venue you have chosen cannot accommodate the number of people who arrive and there is no other space readily available, it is best to let everyone—both the guests and the venue—know as soon as possible. Assign greeters to inform guests of the situation and pass guestbooks around to acknowledge everyone's attendance. You might decide to schedule a second event and gather all the guests' contact information in order to keep them informed.

Conversely, you might be concerned that no one will show up. This is a common fear for those planning services for honorees who have lived in nursing homes for long periods or who have survived many of their friends. Of course you will want to have a memorial service, especially if there is a surviving spouse and children. The service is as much for the survivors as it is a remembrance of the honoree. You will simply need to make sure that the venue is suitable for a small number of attendees. Perhaps there is a restaurant you used to frequent that has a small side room. Even if you decide to hold the service in a house of worship, you can create an intimate atmosphere by making sure guests congregate toward the front. Have ushers follow these instructions for filling the venue: First, block off the front seats as reserved for family members. The ushers should start seating guests one-third of the way from the front, and then fill in the remaining seats before and after those rows as more people arrive. When the front of the church is filled, the later arrivals can sit farther toward the back. If the space is conducive, you can have guests seated on only one side, only utilizing the other side if the first fills. You can also ask people to move closer to the front to fill in the empty spaces. Just be sure the officiant is aware of your concerns and takes them into consideration.

VENUE TIPS

Visiting your prospective venues is one of the easiest ways to avoid unwelcome surprises. Before finalizing a location, take the following into consideration:

- Inquire whether there are any events directly preceding or following your event.
- Ask if you may provide the restrooms with a basket of amenities, including soaps, folding hand towels, and an arrangement of flowers.
- Find out if the venue requires permits for preparing and serving food and alcoholic beverages. Similar permission may also be necessary to use candles, or a fire marshal's presence may be required.
- Inquire if you will need to rent or provide tables and chairs, valet parking drivers, coat-check personnel, or portable toilets.
- Confirm who is responsible for cleaning up after the event.

If there will be food:

- Ensure that your caterer or the venue provides sufficient food for your guests (for bite-size refreshments, estimate six per person).
- Do not serve alcohol without food.
- Have three times the number of glasses as guests to avoid running out.
- Ask if there are any additional costs, such as corkage fees.
- Ask whether you will be allowed to take leftover food or alcohol home.

6
Putting Memories Into Words

Shortly after my father died, we received a phone call from former president Richard Nixon's aide. President Nixon wished to speak at the memorial service. While my siblings and I did not have the most positive associations with the former president and were unsure of his impact on the service, Nixon *had* named my father ambassador to Ireland, and they had a long and rewarding history of working together. We were reminded by another family member that the service was not about us, but rather about our father. Realizing that she was right, we invited Nixon to speak. To our complete surprise, he delivered the eulogy that best captured and honored our father.

Some religious services do not allow for personal eulogies. For these congregations it is the proper way to say good-bye, and it is important to respect that. There are other ways to instill a personal touch without a eulogy, to celebrate the honoree's life by capturing their essence and expressing it.

CAPTURING THE STORIES

Memorial services that include multiple speakers who tell different stories about the honoree from different places and times paint a more complete portrait of an honoree—much more so than any single individual can. The advantage to this approach is that people see the honoree in more depth and gain a greater appreciation of the honoree's life. It can take a community to tell the whole story. This does not mean that a service has to be long, just all-encompassing.

Conversely, deciding what to do when the honoree has expressly stated they do not want anything said at the service or has vetoed having a service at all can be very difficult. In this situation the needs of both the family members and the honoree must be taken into consideration. Here is where preplanning and agreeing on the scope of a service beforehand becomes helpful. For example, if a family gathers stories before they are needed for a memorial service, the honoree might be more willing to have them told. Not knowing what people might say or not wanting to inconvenience someone might be at the root of the negative sentiment expressed about a memorial service.

Stories for the Generations

It is not only fun to tell stories and reminisce, it is also important to have accurate stories to pass along through generations. Once you begin recounting important events and experiences in the lives of your loved ones, you might be surprised by how you and your siblings have very different views of a particular story, and maybe even conflicting details. This is not surprising, given how differently we interpret events at different times in our lives. While younger generations may not be interested in these stories now, they will be as they grow older.

At a memorial service I attended, a family friend and minister spoke about the honoree, a family man with distinctive russet hair. In the audience there were a handful of russet-haired grandbabies, showing how this trait was passed on generation after generation. He picked up each little child one after the other and gently paraded them around the aisles, symbolizing how the honoree's legacy would be carried forward in generations to come. The speaker's reference to them was tastefully and lovingly done.

When people join together to celebrate the life of a loved one, they bring with them knowledge of the honoree that is inherently incomplete—most children will have never known their parents as work colleagues and work colleagues will have never experienced them as parents. More than anything else, stories help to complete the picture from every point of view. One of the primary reasons to have a memorial service is so everyone can join together to share, remember, and enjoy the memories the honoree is leaving behind.

Painting a Positive Picture

Because the eulogy creates a lasting image for those attending the service and helps to ease the pain of loss, it is important to emphasize the positive. This is not the time to bring up resentments, stories of bad judgment, misguided political views, or anything with a negative connotation. Even when cloaked in humor, slights and slurs are not appropriate and accomplish nothing. If the honoree has done something controversial, the memorial service is a place to focus on the positive and to attempt to let go of any ill will.

EULOGIES

There are many ways to remember the honoree with a speech given during the memorial service, and you do not have to be a skilled storyteller to give a meaningful eulogy. While a eulogy based on a story is one of the most popular types, you can also base a eulogy on passages of poetry or prose, an honoree's biography or characteristics, or even just visual symbols with no words at all. Here are a few different types of eulogies; use these ideas as a springboard for your own unique way of expressing your sentiments.

Story Eulogies

A story eulogy uses a specific memory as a foundation for your verbal remembrance. If there is one story or moment that best conveys how you want the honoree to be remembered, this may be the best type of eulogy to write.

Once you have figured out which story you would like to use, think about why it is important and what it says about the honoree. One of the most common mistakes is telling a story that focuses too much on the person telling it—make sure the story highlights the honoree rather than yourself. Only a story that you tell from your heart will sound sincere. While funny, colorful stories will make a eulogy entertaining, it should not be your aim. The goal is to share with the guests the memory of a meaningful good-bye, to build a sense of community, and express your loss in a way that helps others.

Also, the story should have a distinct beginning, middle, and end. Usually there is a lesson learned, an event that changes what people think or do. Keep the story short and intentional, but do include enough background information to make the story understandable and interesting. Make sure the story is relevant to the audience. Keep the eulogy personal. There are many books and websites that offer prewritten eulogies, but the most memorable and touching eulogies are oftentimes the ones told in the speaker's own words. If you have difficulty expressing yourself, then ask for help. Find someone—a clergy member, local journalist, or teacher—who can listen to what you have to say, help you focus on the important points, and organize the information into a speech.

Attribute Eulogy

While capturing an image of an honoree in one word might not work for everyone, it is an interesting way to distill a remembrance down to its most vital parts. A eulogy built around one word or characteristic will be more focused and intense. For example, if the honoree embodied all the attributes in the Boy Scout's Oath, divide the most important ones among multiple speakers, and have each one talk about how that specific characteristic related to the honoree. However, most people will only be able to remember five characteristics at most—any more than that will be lost, so be concise and intentional when choosing which attributes to focus on.

Biographical Eulogy

A biographical eulogy is framed by the honoree's chronological history and serves as a powerful way to celebrate who the honoree was by what he or she did. If you know that many of the guests at the service will be attending in support of a friend or relative of the honoree, then a biographical eulogy can be a good way to unite all the guests, in a way that a story or attribute eulogy might not.

When preparing a biographical eulogy, remember that it is not necessary to include every detail of the honoree's life—it is more important to highlight those accomplishments that best celebrate him or her while providing a well-rounded picture. A biographical description of an honoree's life may also be the way the honoree wishes to be remembered. While this can be one of the simplest eulogies to write for someone who knew the honoree well, remember that this type of eulogy will have more meaning if you include personal details along with biographical facts. Often these details are what make the biography come to life and the parts that most truly express the nature of the honoree.

Open Mic Eulogy

In some cases speeches are not planned—instead, guests are invited to say what they wish, either planned or unrehearsed, in front of the group. This type of remembrance is often used because it is easy and takes no planning. However, there is a risk that an unskilled (yet well-meaning) speaker will speak for too long, focus on him- or herself rather than the honoree, or say something inappropriate. Consequently, many people find that this is too important an occasion to leave to chance, and feel that coordinated, preplanned speeches are more appropriate.

Symbolic Eulogy

For some honorees, no words need to be said. This may be a time where you take a more symbolic approach to a eulogy. You may select people to light candles and recite poems or quotations that highlight the attributes of an honoree. You may wish to sit in silence or use a guided meditation in remembrance. Music might work best. There is no right or wrong way to remember someone. The point is simply to capture the heart and essence of the honoree.

SETTING THE TONE

One of the first people to speak at my uncle's service asked, "Let me see a show of hands. Who among you ever rode in a car when Richard Moore was driving?" My uncle was a notoriously poor driver; his focus was on everything except the road ahead. The audience erupted in laughter and you could feel the tension release.

Memorial services and celebrations can be relaxed, personal, and friendly—if that is what suits the honoree. It can be enormously relieving for everybody if a story is told to set people at ease. However, for a person more guided by protocol and never irreverent, this may be an incongruous approach. A more elegant or sophisticated tone might be more appropriate. It is equally important to set the tone for what should not be said. If the honoree has skeletons in the closet, the memorial service is not the time to bring them out, not even humorously. Avoid stories that put the honoree in a bad light or cross the line between slightly irreverent and slandering.

A good friend shared with me an experience she had at a memorial service. As the speakers came forward it soon became apparent that the honoree had many romantic relationships in her life, and that these suitors were still in competition! Knowing who was going to say what before the service could have resulted in a more balanced, respectful tone.

A NOTE ON SPEAKERS

Choose your speakers carefully. Not everyone who has something important to say is a good speaker. A good speaker is someone who makes a story heartfelt and who speaks as if they are talking only to you. Look for people who know the honoree and have good speaking skills; oftentimes business people or group leaders are strong public speakers. It is okay to feed stories to good speakers as long as you acknowledge that at the outset. You can also ask a professional or highly regarded speaker to speak at the memorial service if there is an appropriate connection. For example, you could ask a Nobel Prize–winning poet from the honoree's college to speak. You might be surprised by the response. On the other hand, as much as you prepare beforehand you may find you have a speaker with an agenda. It is up to you to protect the honoree from any negativity. If a subject is broached that should not be, you should be ready to curtail the speech—everyone will understand.

If there is someone who does want to speak and for whatever reason should not, you can find another role for him or her to play in the memorial service.

Perhaps they can read a poem or quotation, or participate in a way that does not involve public speaking at all. Honor the fact that the person wants to contribute, and find the most appropriate way to do so.

Give the speakers guidelines and let them know how long to talk. (Generally, leaving people wanting more is better than going on too long.) Asking three to four people to speak for three minutes each is ideal. A single typed page with three hundred words takes approximately five minutes to deliver. If there is only one speaker, then a longer time, maybe ten to fifteen minutes, could be appropriate depending on the overall length of the service.

A potential speaker may have a wonderful story or sentiment to convey, but knows that the emotion of the moment will make it impossible to actually speak at the service. In this case, a spouse, friend, or clergy member may be the better person to deliver the speech. While everyone understands the difficulty of surmounting the emotion, a surrogate speaker can help ease some tension and emotion. The author of the speech can stand or sit near the speaker, or can be ceremoniously escorted to a front row seat for the presentation.

Readings

7

Passages and Poetry

The right quotation, poem, or passage spoken as a tribute to an honoree can add tremendous significance to the memorial service and the memories evoked there. Few people are professional writers and fewer still are poets; finding the expressive words needed at a time of loss makes it even more difficult. Yet the most sincere and true words will come from those closest to the honoree. Of course, some of the best quotations will be those that come directly from the honoree and are remembered by friends and family. If someone has a frequent pet phrase or is known for an inspirational saying, those quotations will ring the truest and should be featured. If you don't have any personal quotations or original writing, look to literature for a quotation, poem, or passage that captures the essence of the honoree's character and touches on at least one of these themes:

1. A reflection of what the honoree would say to those attending the service
2. A description of a particular characteristic of the honoree
3. A reflection of what those in attendance would say to the honoree

It is difficult to find quotations that elicit noteworthy memories without being sad or overly sentimental. Traditional services call upon passages easily extracted from their religious sources, and they run the risk of losing their true meaning and impact because of the familiarity and lack of context. Words about death are too often chosen over complimentary words about the honoree. The right words will help people relate to the best characteristics, wisdom, or personal interests of the honoree, and bring the best memories forward.

There are many different ways quotations, poetry, and passages can be used, but be careful not to overuse them—let personal stories dominate. One poignant quotation or poem will have more meaning than a clutter of them. If there is a special meaning for a chosen passage, mention it during the service, especially if it was selected by the honoree. Following is a selection of quotations, poems, and passages that can help guide you in making your own choices.

SHORT QUOTATIONS

Short quotations used on a program or beneath a photo can add impact, dignity, or help characterize the honoree, even in a light-hearted or humorous way. They can be inscribed on a bookmark, the service program, or even on napkins, matchbooks, a poster, or other displays about the honoree.

With Us Always

"Are we going to be friends forever?"
asked Piglet. "Even longer," Pooh answered.
— A. A. Milne

Praising what is lost
Makes the remembrance dear.
— William Shakespeare

The soul of man is immortal and imperishable.
— Plato

A Person of Character

He was a man, take him for all in all,
I shall not look upon his like again.
— William Shakespeare

His life was gentle and the elements
So mixed in him that nature might stand up
And say to all the world, "This was a man."
— William Shakespeare

Personality can open doors, but only character can keep them open.
— Elmer G. Letterman

People grow through experience if they meet life honestly and courageously.
This is how character is built.
— Eleanor Roosevelt

Character cannot be developed in ease and quiet. Only through experience
of trial and suffering can the soul be strengthened, ambition inspired, and
success achieved.
— Helen Keller

Creativity

One of the advantages of being disorderly is that one is constantly making
exciting discoveries.
— A. A. Milne

Human salvation lies in the hands of the creatively maladjusted.
— Martin Luther King Jr.

Creativity can solve almost any problem. The creative act, the defeat of habit by originality, overcomes everything.
— George Lois

To live a creative life, we must lose our fear of being wrong.
— Joseph Chilton Pearce

Creativity is allowing yourself to make mistakes. Art is knowing which ones to keep.
— Scott Adams

Every time we say, "Let there be!" in any form, something happens.
— Stella Terrill Mann

Creativity is . . . seeing something that doesn't exist already. You need to find out how you can bring it into being and that way be a playmate with God.
— Michele Shea

Curiosity and a Love for Learning

The love of learning, the sequestered nooks,
And all the sweet serenity of books.
— Henry Wadsworth Longfellow

In the highest civilization, the book is still the highest delight. He who has once known its satisfactions is provided with a resource against calamity.
— Ralph Waldo Emerson

Knowing I lov'd my books, he furnish'd me
From mine own library with volumes that
I prize above my dukedom.
— William Shakespeare

The important thing is not to stop questioning. Curiosity has its own reason for existing. One cannot help but be in awe when he contemplates the mysteries of eternity, of life, of the marvelous structure of reality. It is enough if one tries merely to comprehend a little of this mystery every day. Never lose a holy curiosity.
— Albert Einstein

The wisest mind has something yet to learn.
— George Santayana

Science is organized knowledge. Wisdom is organized life.
— Immanuel Kant

Men are wise in proportion, not to their experience,
but to their capacity for experience.
— James Boswell

We don't receive wisdom; we must discover it for ourselves after
a journey that no one can take for us or spare us.
— Marcel Proust

Wisdom outweighs any wealth.
— Sophocles

Art and the Artist

Art is born of the observation and investigation of nature.
— Cicero

Every artist dips his brush in his own soul, and paints his own nature into his pictures.
— Henry Ward Beecher

Painting is an attempt to come to terms with life. There are as many solutions as there are human beings.
— George Tooker

Through all the world there goes one long cry from the heart of the artist: Give me leave to do my utmost.
— Isak Dinesen

We must never forget that art is not a form of propaganda; it is a form of truth.
— John F. Kennedy

The creation of art is not the fulfillment of a need but the creation of a need. The world never needed Beethoven's Fifth Symphony until he created it. Now we could not live without it.
— Louis I. Kahn

Painting is silent poetry, and poetry is painting with the gift of speech.
— Simonides

Music and the Musician

I merely took the energy it takes to pout and wrote some blues.
— Duke Ellington

Among all men on the earth bards have a share of honor and reverence, because the muse has taught them songs and loves the race of bards.
— Homer

Ah, music. A magic beyond all we do here!
— J. K. Rowling

My heart, which is so full to overflowing, has often been solaced and refreshed by music when sick and weary.
— Martin Luther

Music is the wine that fills the cup of silence.
— Robert Fripp

Music has charms to soothe the savage breast
To soften rocks, or bend a knotted oak.
— William Congreve

If music be the food of love, play on.
— William Shakespeare

A bird does not sing because it has an answer. It sings because it has a song.
— Chinese Proverb

Dance and the Dancer

There was a star danced,
and under that was I born.
—William Shakespeare

Dance is the hidden language of the soul.
— Martha Graham

The dance is a poem of which each movement is a word.
— Mata Hari

Dance like no one is watching. Love like you've never been hurt. Sing like no one is listening. Live like it's heaven on Earth.
— William Purkey

For what is it to die, but to stand in the sun and melt into the wind? And when the Earth has claimed our limbs, then we shall truly dance.
— Kahlil Gibran

I am lost, and I rejoice in the openness. I cannot decide where to go, so for now, I will dance where I am and be. There is no goal, no destination, just wilderness and life and being. I sing and dance and live in the wilderness, and I am home.
— Tziporah

Let your life lightly dance on the edges of Time like dew on the tip of a leaf.
— Rabindranath Tagore

Human beings, vegetables, or cosmic dust, we all dance to a mysterious tune intoned in the distance by an invisible player.
— Albert Einstein

Gardens and the Gardener

Those who bring sunshine to the lives of others cannot keep it from themselves.
— J. M. Barrie

Let us be grateful to people who make us happy; they are the charming gardeners who make our souls blossom.
— Marcel Proust

The comfortable and comforting people are those who look upon the bright side of life; gathering roses and sunshine and making the worst that happens seem the best.
— Dorothy Dix

A garden is always a series of losses set against a few triumphs, like life itself.
— May Sarton

All that in this delightful garden grows, should happy be, and have immortal bliss.
— Edmund Spenser

If you have a mind at peace, and a heart that cannot harden,
Go find a door that opens wide upon a lovely garden.
— Anonymous

Our bodies are our gardens, to which our wills are gardeners.
— William Shakespeare

The world is so empty if one thinks only of mountains, rivers, and cities;
but to know someone here and there who thinks and feels with us, and though
distant, is close to us in spirit—this makes the earth for us an
inhabited garden.
— Johann von Goethe

The desert shall rejoice and blossom;
like the crocus it shall blossom abundantly,
and rejoice with joy and singing.
— Isaiah 35: 1–2

He that has two cakes of bread,
let him sell one of them for a Narcissus flower,
for bread is food for the body,
but the Narcissus is food of the soul.
— The Qur'an

Look at the trees, look at the birds, look at the clouds, look at the stars . . .
and if you have eyes you will be able to see that the whole existence is joyful.
Everything is simply happy. Trees are happy for no reason; they are not going

to become prime ministers or presidents and they are not going to become rich and they will never have any bank balance. Look at the flowers—for no reason. It is simply unbelievable how happy flowers are.
— Osho

A man is successful who has lived well, laughed often, and loved much, who has gained the respect of intelligent men and the love of children; who has filled his niche and accomplished his task; who leaves the world better than he found it, whether by an improved poppy, a perfect poem, or a rescued soul; who never lacked appreciation of earth's beauty or failed to express it; who looked for the best in others and gave the best he had.
— Robert Louis Stevenson

At Christmas I no more desire a rose
Than wish a snow in May's new-fangled mirth;
But like of each thing that in season grows.
— William Shakespeare

God gave us memory so that we might have roses in December.
— J. M. Barrie

Sports

Golf is so popular simply because it is the best game in the world at which to be bad.
— A. A. Milne

You owe it to yourself to be the best you can possibly be—in baseball and in life.
— Pete Rose

Sports serve society by providing vivid examples of excellence.
— George F. Will

For when the One Great Scorer comes
To write against your name,
He marks—not that you won or lost—
But how you played the game.
— Grantland Rice

Sports do not build character. They reveal it.
— Heywood Hale Broun

A good hockey player plays where the puck is. A great hockey player plays
where the puck is going to be.
— Wayne Gretzky

Small in Stature

Though she be but little she be fierce.
— William Shakespeare

Friendship

The life I touch for good or ill will touch another life, and that in turn another,
until who knows where the trembling stops or in what far place my touch will
be felt.
— Frederick Buechner

A friend is someone who knows the song in your heart and can sing it back to
you when you have forgotten the words.
— Unknown

The most beautiful discovery true friends make is that they can grow sepa-
rately without growing apart.
— Elisabeth Foley

Truly great friends are hard to find, difficult to leave, and impossible to forget.
— Unknown

Don't cry because it's over. Smile because it happened.
— Dr. Seuss

Life is partly what we make it, and partly what it is made by the friends we choose.
— Tennessee Williams

When we honestly ask ourselves which person in our lives means the most to us, we often find that it is those who, instead of giving much advice, solutions, or cures, have chosen rather to share our pain and touch our wounds with a gentle and tender hand. The friend who can be silent with us in a moment of despair or confusion, who can stay with us in an hour of grief and bereavement, who can tolerate not knowing, not curing, not healing and face with us the reality of our powerlessness, that is a friend who cares.
— Henri Nouwen

It's the friends you can call up at 4 a.m. that matter.
— Marlene Dietrich

Each friend represents a world in us, a world possibly not born until they arrive, and it is only by this meeting that a new world is born.
— Anaïs Nin

What is a friend? A single soul dwelling in two bodies.
— Aristotle

Friendship is born at that moment when one person says to another: "What! You, too? I thought I was the only one."
— C. S. Lewis

Those truly linked don't need correspondence. When they meet again after many years apart, their friendship is as true as ever.
— Deng Ming-Dao

A faithful friend is a strong defense: and he that hath found such an one hath found a treasure.
— Ecclesiasticus 6:14

It is not so much our friends' help that helps us as the confident knowledge that they will help us.
— Epicurus

The bird a nest
the spider a web
Man friendship.
— William Blake

Caring for Others

Only a life lived for others is worth living.
— Albert Einstein

Weeds are flowers too, once you get to know them.
— A. A. Milne

I am of the opinion that my life belongs to the community, and as long as I live it is my privilege to do for it whatever I can.
— George Bernard Shaw

Happiness is not so much in having as sharing. We make a living by what we get, but we make a life by what we give.
— Norman MacEwan

The purpose of life is a life of purpose.
— Robert Byrne

An individual has not started living until he can rise above the narrow confines of his individualistic concerns to the broader concerns of all humanity.
— Martin Luther King Jr.

The person who tries to live alone will not succeed as a human being. His heart withers if it does not answer another heart. His mind shrinks away if he hears only the echoes of his own thoughts and finds no other inspiration.
— Pearl S. Buck

A bone to the dog is not charity. Charity is the bone shared with the dog, when you are just as hungry as the dog.
— Jack London

The only gift is a portion of thyself.
— Ralph Waldo Emerson

Trail Blazing

This above all: to thine own self be true,
And it must follow, as the night the day,
Thou canst not then be false to any man.
— William Shakespeare

Do not go where the path may lead, go instead where there is no path and leave a trail.
— Ralph Waldo Emerson

Insist on yourself; never imitate . . . . Every great man is unique.
— Ralph Waldo Emerson

The wisest men follow their own direction.
— Euripides

You see things; and you say, "Why?" But I dream things that never were; and I say, "Why not?"
— George Bernard Shaw

One ship sails East,
And another West,
By the self-same winds that blow,
'Tis the set of the sails
And not the gales,
That tells the way we go.
Like the winds of the sea
Are the waves of time,
As we journey along through life,
'Tis the set of the soul,
That determines the goal,
And not the calm or the strife.
— Ella Wheeler Wilcox

No bird soars too high, if he soars with his own wings.
— William Blake

The universe will reward you for taking risks on its behalf.
— Shakti Gawain

Life Well-Lived

And we should consider every day lost on which we have not danced at least once. And we should call every truth false which was not accompanied by at least one laugh.
— Friedrich Nietzsche

What is the meaning of life? To be happy and useful.
— the Dalai Lama

Thousands of candles can be lit from a single candle, and the life of the candle will not be shortened. Happiness never decreases by being shared.
— Buddha

Live your life and forget your age.
— Norman Vincent Peale

What we call the secret of happiness is no more a secret than our willingness to choose life.
— Leo Buscaglia

And in the end, it's not the years in your life that count. It's the life in your years.
— Abraham Lincoln

My candle burns at both its ends;
It will not last the night;
But ah, my foes, and oh, my friends—
It gives a lovely light.
— Edna St. Vincent Millay

There was never yet an uninteresting life. Such a thing is an impossibility. Inside of the dullest exterior there is a drama, a comedy, and a tragedy.
— Mark Twain

Life begets life. Energy creates energy. It is by spending oneself that one becomes rich.
— Sarah Bernhardt

These, then, are my last words to you: Be not afraid of life. Believe that life is worth living, and your belief will help create that fact.
— William James

Struggling Against Adversity

The ultimate measure of a man is not where he stands in moments of comfort and convenience, but where he stands at times of challenge and controversy.
— Martin Luther King Jr.

*It is worthwhile to live
and fight courageously
for sacred ideals.*
— Norbert Capek

Only when we are no longer afraid do we begin to live.
— Dorothy Thompson

Conscience is the root of all true courage; if a man would be brave let him obey his conscience.
— James Freeman Clarke

We who lived in concentration camps can remember the men who walked through the huts comforting others, giving away their last piece of bread. They may have been few in number, but they offer sufficient proof that everything can be taken from a man but one thing: the last of the human freedoms—to choose one's attitude in any given set of circumstances, to choose one's own way.
— Viktor Frankl

The experience of democracy is like the experience of life itself—always changing, infinite in its variety, sometimes turbulent, and all the more valuable for having been tested by adversity.
— Jimmy Carter

When at some future date the high court of history sits in judgment on each of us . . . our success or failure, in whatever office we may hold, will be measured by the answers to four questions: First, were we truly men of

courage . . . ? Secondly, were we truly men of judgment . . . ? Third, were
we truly men of integrity . . . ? Finally, were we truly men of dedication . . . ?
— John F. Kennedy

Eternal vigilance is the price of liberty.
— Wendell Phillips

If abuses are destroyed, man must destroy them. If slaves are freed, man must
free them. If new truths are discovered, man must discover them. If the naked
are clothed; if the hungry are fed; if justice is done; if labor is rewarded; if
superstition is driven from the mind; if the defenseless are protected, and if
the right finally triumphs, all must be the work of man. The grand victories of
the future must be won by man, and by man alone.
— Robert Ingersoll

Nature

When Nature has work to be done, she creates a genius to do it.
— Ralph Waldo Emerson

When it's over, I want to say: all my life
I was a bride married to amazement.
I was the bridegroom, taking the world into my arms.
— Mary Oliver

The goal of life is living in agreement with nature.
— Zeno

The sun, with all those planets revolving around it and dependent upon it,
can still ripen a bunch of grapes as if it had nothing else in the universe to do.
— Galileo Galilei

Birth, life, and death—each took place on the hidden side of a leaf.
— Toni Morrison

To see a world in a grain of sand,
And a heaven in a wild flower,
Hold infinity in the palm of your hand,
And eternity in an hour.
— William Blake

One of the most important resources that a garden makes available for use, is the gardener's own body. A garden gives the body the dignity of working in its own support. It is a way of rejoining the human race.
— Wendell Berry

All I have seen teaches me to trust the creator for all I have not seen.
— Ralph Waldo Emerson

Let us not forget that the cultivation of the earth is the most important labor of man. When tillage begins, other arts will follow. The farmers, therefore, are the founders of civilization.
— Daniel Webster

Inner Beauty

The best part of beauty is that which no picture can express.
— Francis Bacon

To affect the quality of the day, that is the highest of arts.
— Henry David Thoreau

True wealth is not measured by money or status or power. It is measured by the legacy we leave behind for those we love and those we inspire.
— Cesar Chavez

A life spent worthily should be measured by a nobler line—by deeds, not years.
— Richard Brinsley Sheridan

Some people come into our lives and quickly go. Others stay awhile, make footprints on our hearts, and we are never, ever the same.
— Unknown

As we grow old . . . the beauty steals inward.
— Ralph Waldo Emerson

Teaching

Teachers believe they have a gift for giving; it drives them with the same irrepressible drive that drives others to create a work of art or a market or a building.
— A. Bartlett Giamatti

The teacher's task is not to implant facts but to place the subject to be learned in front of the learner and, through sympathy, emotion, imagination and patience, to awaken in the learner the restless drive for answers and insights which enlarge the personal life and give it meaning.
— Nathan Pusey

A teacher affects eternity; he can never tell where his influence stops.
— Henry Brooks Adams

It takes a village to raise a child . . . a timeless reminder that children will only thrive if their families thrive and if the whole of society cares enough to provide for them.
— Hillary Rodham Clinton

The job of an educator is to teach students to see the vitality in themselves.
— Joseph Campbell

What greater or better gift can we offer the republic than to teach and instruct our youth?
— Marcus T. Cicero

It is the supreme art of the teacher to awaken joy in creative expression and knowledge.
— Albert Einstein

You cannot teach a man anything; you can only help him find it within himself.
— Galielo Galilei

Teachers open the door. You enter by yourself.
— Chinese proverb

Good teaching is one-fourth preparation and three-fourths theater.
— Gail Godwin

Education's purpose is to replace an empty mind with an open one.
— Malcolm Forbes

The very spring and root of honesty and virtue lie in good education.
— Plutarch

Parenting

Making the decision to have a child—it's momentous. It is to decide forever to have your heart go walking around outside your body.
— Elizabeth Stone

Good parents give their children Roots and Wings. Roots to know where home is, wings to fly away and exercise what's been taught them.
— Jonas Salk

The longer we live, and the more we think, the higher the value we learn to put on the friendship and tenderness of parents and of friends.
— Samuel Johnson

I've been very blessed. My parents always told me I could be anything I wanted. When you grow up in a household like that, you learn to believe in yourself.
— Rick Schroeder

My mother had a great deal of trouble with me, but I think she enjoyed it.
— Mark Twain

The most important thing she'd learned over the years was that there was no way to be a perfect mother and a million ways to be a good one.
— Jill Churchill

The art of mothering is to teach the art of living to children.
— Elain Heffner

A mother is not a person to lean on, but a person to make leaning unnecessary.
— Dorothy C. Fisher

Love

There is no remedy for love but to love more.
— Henry David Thoreau

And when love speaks, the voice of all the gods makes heaven drowsy with the harmony.
— William Shakespeare

Shall I compare thee to a summer's day?
Thou art more lovely and more temperate.
— William Shakespeare

A successful marriage requires falling in love many times,
always with the same person.
— Mignon McLaughlin

And did you get what you
wanted from this life, even so?
I did.
And what did you want?
To call myself beloved, to feel myself
beloved on the earth.
— Raymond Carver

To love deeply in one direction makes us more loving in all others.
— Anne-Sophie Swetchine

To love and be loved is to feel the sun from both sides.
— David Viscott

Love is everything it's cracked up to be . . . . It really is worth fighting for, being
brave for, risking everything for.
— Erica Jong

I pay very little regard . . . to what any young person says on the subject of
marriage. If they profess a disinclination for it, I only set it down that they
have not yet seen the right person.
— Jane Austen

Love is, above all else, the gift of oneself.
— Jean Anouilh

To love is to receive a glimpse of heaven.
— Karen Sunde

For one human being to love another; that is perhaps the most difficult of all our tasks, the ultimate, the last test and proof, the work for which all other work is but preparation.
— Rainer Maria Rilke

Before I met my husband, I'd never fallen in love. I'd stepped in it a few times.
— Rita Rudner

One word frees us of all the weight and pain of life: That word is love.
— Sophocles

There is no fear in love; but perfect love casts out fear.
— 1 John 4:18

POETRY

The essence of poetry is that much is said in very few words. Just like using symbols and colors to speak to all of the senses, poetry too can have many levels of meaning. Choose poems that speak to the life the honoree lived or your feelings about the honoree. If a poem's significance is not obvious to all those attending, be sure to explain.

There are many ways to use poetry throughout the memorial service. You do not even have to include the whole poem, especially if it is long—just one notable stanza will serve as a reminder for a familiar poem and might be more effective. Also consider having a musical background during the reading. A soft flute, acoustic guitar, violin, or cello can all create more depth. You can also include poems in programs as a memento for those attending, use them as texts for a photographic display in video, or print them on postcards or bookmarks. Here are some examples of poems appropriate for memorial services.

Patriotism

High Flight
by John Gillespie Magee Jr.

Oh! I have slipped the surly bonds of Earth
And danced the skies on laughter-silvered wings;
Sunward I've climbed, and joined the tumbling mirth
Of sun-split clouds,—and done a hundred things
You have not dreamed of—wheeled and soared and swung
High in the sunlit silence. Hov'ring there,
I've chased the shouting wind along, and flung
My eager craft through footless halls of air . . .

Up, up the long, delirious burning blue
I've topped the wind-swept heights with easy grace
Where never lark nor ever eagle flew—
And, while with silent lifting mind I've trod
The high untrespassed sanctity of space,
Put out my hand, and touched the face of God.

Adieu to a Solider
by Walt Whitman

Adieu, O soldier!
You of the rude campaigning, (which we shared,)
The rapid march, the life of the camp,
The hot contention of opposing fronts—the long maneuver,
Red battles with their slaughter,—the stimulus—the strong, terrific game,
Spell of all brave and manly hearts—the trains of Time through you,
     and like of you, all fill'd,
With war, and war's expression.

Adieu, dear comrade!
Your mission is fulfill'd—but I, more warlike,
Myself, and this contentious soul of mine,

Still on our own campaigning bound,
Through untried roads, with ambushes, opponents lined,
Through many a sharp defeat and many a crisis—often baffled,
Here marching, ever marching on, a war fight out—aye here,
To fiercer, weightier battles give expression.

Prayer of a Soldier in France
by Joyce Kilmer

My shoulders ache beneath my pack
(Lie easier, Cross, upon His back).

I march with feet that burn and smart
(Tread, Holy Feet, upon my heart).

Men shout at me who may not speak
(They scourged Thy back and smote Thy cheek).

I may not lift a hand to clear
My eyes of salty drops that sear.
(Then shall my fickle soul forget
Thy Agony of Bloody Sweat?)
My rifle hand is stiff and numb
(From Thy pierced palm red rivers come).

Lord, Thou didst suffer more for me
Than all the hosts of land and sea.

So let me render back again
This millionth of Thy gift. Amen.

In Former Songs
by Walt Whitman

In former songs Pride have I sung, and Love, and passionate, joyful Life,
But here I twine the strands of Patriotism and Death.

And now, Life, Pride, Love, Patriotism and Death,
To you, O Freedom, purport of all!
(You that elude me most—refusing to be caught in songs of mine,)
I offer all to you.

'Tis not for nothing, Death,
I sound out you, and words of you, with daring tone—embodying you,
In my new Democratic chants—keeping you for a close,
For last impregnable retreat—a citadel and tower,
For my last stand—my pealing, final cry.

I Hear America Singing
by Walt Whitman
I hear America singing, the varied carols I hear;
Those of mechanics—each one singing his, as it should be, blithe
    and strong;
The carpenter singing his, as he measures his plank or beam
The mason singing his, as he makes ready for work,
    or leaves off work;
The boatman singing what belongs to him in his boat—
    the deckhand singing on the steamboat deck;
The shoemaker singing as he sits on his bench—
    the hatter singing as he stands;
The wood-cutter's song—the ploughboy's, on his way
    in the morning, or at noon intermission, or at sundown;
The delicious singing of the mother—or of the young wife
    at work—or of the girl sewing or washing—
Each singing what belongs to her, and to none else;
The day what belongs to the day—At night,
    the party of young fellows, robust, friendly,
Singing, with open mouths, their strong melodious songs.

Sonnet XVIII
by William Shakespeare
Shall I compare thee to a summer's day?
Thou art more lovely and more temperate:
Rough winds do shake the darling buds of May,
And summer's lease hath all too short a date:
Sometime too hot the eye of heaven shines,
And often is his gold complexion dimm'd;
And every fair from fair sometime declines,
By chance or nature's changing course untrimm'd;
But thy eternal summer shall not fade
Nor lose possession of that fair thou owest;
Nor shall Death brag thou wander'st in his shade,
When in eternal lines to time thou growest:
So long as men can breathe or eyes can see,
So long lives this and this gives life to thee.

Something Childish, but Very Natural
by Samuel Taylor Coleridge
If I had but two little wings
And were a little feathery bird,
To you I'd fly, my dear!
But thoughts like these are idle things,
And I stay here.

But in my sleep to you I fly:
I'm always with you in my sleep!
The world is all one's own.
But then one wakes, and where am I?
All, all alone.

Sleep stays not, though a monarch bids:
So I love to wake ere break of day:
For though my sleep be gone,
Yet while 'tis dark, one shuts one's lids,
And still dreams on.

Remember
by Christina Georgina Rossetti
Remember me when I am gone away,
Gone far away into the silent land;
When you can no more hold me by the hand,
Not I half turning to go yet turning stay.
Remember me when no more day by day
You tell me of our future that you plann'd:
Only remember me; you understand
It will be too late to counsel then or pray.
Yet if you should forget me for a while
And afterwards remember, do not grieve:
For if the darkness and corruption leave
A vestige of the thoughts that once I had,
Better by far you should forget and smile
Than that you should remember and be sad.

Love's Lantern (For Aline)
by Joyce Kilmer
Because the road was steep and long
And through a dark and lonely land,
God set upon my lips a song
And put a lantern in my hand.
Through miles on weary miles of night
That stretch relentless in my way
My lantern burns serene and white,
An unexhausted cup of day.
O golden lights and lights like wine,

How dim your boasted splendors are.
Behold this little lamp of mine;
It is more starlike than a star!

Riches
by Sara Teasdale
I have no riches but my thoughts,
Yet these are wealth enough for me;
My thoughts of you are golden coins
Stamped in the mint of memory;

And I must spend them all in song,
For thoughts, as well as gold, must be
Left on the hither side of death
To gain their immortality.

For Those Who Have Changed Us

The Years
by Sara Teasdale
To-night I close my eyes and see
A strange procession passing me—
The years before I saw your face
Go by me with a wistful grace;
They pass, the sensitive, shy years,
As one who strives to dance, half blind with tears.

The years went by and never knew
That each one brought me nearer you;
Their path was narrow and apart
And yet it led me to your heart—
Oh, sensitive, shy years, oh, lonely years,
That strove to sing with voices drowned in tears.

Before Knowledge
by Thomas Hardy

When I walked roseless tracks and wide,
Ere dawned your date for meeting me,
O why did you not cry Halloo
Across the stretch between, and say:

"We move, while years as yet divide,
On closing lines which—though it be
You know me not nor I know you—
Will intersect and join some day!"

Then well I had borne
Each scraping thorn;
But the winters froze,
And grew no rose;
No bridge bestrode
The gap at all;
No shape you showed,
And I heard no call!

Sonnet XLI
by Elizabeth Barrett Browning

I thank all who have loved me in their hearts,
With thanks and love from mine. Deep thanks to all
Who paused a little near the prison-wall
To hear my music in its louder parts
Ere they went onward, each one to the mart's
Or temple's occupation, beyond call.
But thou, who, in my voice's sink and fall
When the sob took it, thy divinest Art's
Own instrument didst drop down at thy foot
To hearken what I said between my tears, . . .
Instruct me how to thank thee! Oh, to shoot

My soul's full meaning into future years,

That they should lend it utterance, and salute

Love that endures, from Life that disappears!

Sonnet XXXVIII

by Elizabeth Barrett Browning

First time he kissed me, he but only kissed

The fingers of this hand wherewith I write;

And ever since, it grew more clean and white.

Slow to world-greetings, quick with its "O, list,"

When the angels speak. A ring of amethyst

I could not wear here, plainer to my sight,

Than that first kiss. The second passed in height

The first, and sought the forehead, and half missed,

Half falling on the hair. O beyond meed!

That was the chrism of love, which love's own crown,

With sanctifying sweetness, did precede.

The third upon my lips was folded down

In perfect, purple state; since when, indeed,

I have been proud and said, "My love, my own."

Sonnet CXVI

by William Shakespeare

Let me not to the marriage of true minds

Admit impediments. Love is not love

Which alters when it alteration finds,

Or bends with the remover to remove:

O no! it is an ever-fixed mark

That looks on tempests and is never shaken;

It is the star to every wandering bark,

Whose worth's unknown, although his height be taken.

Love's not Time's fool, though rosy lips and cheeks
Within his bending sickle's compass come:
Love alters not with his brief hours and weeks,
But bears it out even to the edge of doom.
If this be error and upon me proved,
I never writ, nor no man ever loved.

Sonnet XXVII
by Elizabeth Barrett Browning
My own Beloved, who hast lifted me
From this drear flat of earth where I was thrown,
And, in betwixt the languid ringlets, blown
A life-breath, till the forehead hopefully
Shines out again, as all the angels see,
Before thy saving kiss! My own, my own,
Who camest to me when the world was gone,
And I who looked for only God, found thee!
I find thee; I am safe, and strong, and glad.
As one who stands in dewless asphodel
Looks backward on the tedious time he had
In the upper life,—so I, with bosom-swell,
Make witness, here, between the good and bad,
That Love, as strong as Death, retrieves as well.

How Do I Love Thee?
by Elizabeth Barrett Browning
How do I love thee? Let me count the ways.
I love thee to the depth and breadth and height
My soul can reach, when feeling out of sight
For the ends of Being and ideal Grace.
I love thee to the level of every day's
Most quiet need, by sun and candlelight.
I love thee freely, as men strive for Right;
I love thee purely, as they turn from Praise.

I love with a passion put to use
In my old griefs, and with my childhood's faith.
I love thee with a love I seemed to lose
With my lost saints,—I love thee with the breath,
Smiles, tears, of all my life!—and, if God choose,
I shall but love thee better after death.

The Song of Wandering Aengus
by William Bulter Yeats
I went out to the hazel wood,
Because a fire was in my head,
And cut and peeled a hazel wand,
And hooked a berry to a thread;
And when white moths were on the wing,
And moth-like stars were flickering out,
I dropped the berry in a stream
And caught a little silver trout.
When I had laid it on the floor
I went to blow the fire a-flame,
But something rustled on the floor,
And someone called me by my name:
It had become a glimmering girl
With apple blossom in her hair
Who called me by my name and ran
And faded through the brightening air.

Though I am old with wandering
Through hollow lands and hilly lands
I will find out where she has gone,
And kiss her lips and take her hands;
And walk among long dappled grass,
And pluck till time and times are done
The silver apples of the moon,
The golden apples of the sun.

The Net
by Sara Teasdale

I made you many and many a song,
Yet never one told all you are—
It was as though a net of words
Were flung to catch a star;

It was as though I curved my hand
And dipped sea-water eagerly,
Only to find it lost the blue
Dark splendor of the sea.

To Merry Margaret Hussey
by John Skelton

Merry Margaret
   As midsummer flower,
   Gentle as falcon
   Or hawk of the tower;
With solace and gladness,
Much mirth and no madness,
All good and no badness;
   So joyously,
   So maidenly,
   So womanly
   Her demeaning
   In every thing
   Far, far passing
   That I can indite
   Or suffice to write
Of Merry Margaret,
As midsummer flower,
Gentle as falcon
Or hawk of the tower.
As patient and still

And as full of good will

As fair Isaphill,

Coliander,

Sweet pomander,

Good Casander;

Steadfast of thought,

Well made, well wrought.

Far may be sought

Ere than ye can find

So courteous, so kind

As merry Margaret,

This midsummer flower,

Gentle as falcon

Or hawk of the tower.

Lochinvar

by Sir Walter Scott

Oh! young Lochinvar is come out of the west,

Through all the wide Border his steed was the best;

And save his good broadsword he weapons had none.

He rode all unarmed and he rode all alone.

So faithful in love and so dauntless in war,

There never was knight like the young Lochinvar.

He stayed not for brake and be stopped not for stone,

He swam the Eske river where ford there was none,

But ere be alighted at Netherby gate

The bride had consented, the gallant came late;

For a laggard in love and a dastard in war

Was to wed the fair Ellen of brave Lochinvar.

So boldly he entered the Netherby Hall,

Among bridesmen, and kinsmen, and brothers, and all:

Then spoke the bride's father, his hand on his sword,—

For the poor craven bridegroom said never a word,—
"Oh! come ye in peace here, or come ye in war,
Or to dance at our bridal, young Lord Lochinvar?"

"I long wooed your daughter, my suit you denied;
Love swells like the Solway, but ebbs like its tide—
And now am I come, with this lost love of mine
To lead but one measure, drink one cup of wine.
There are maidens in Scotland more lovely by far,
That would gladly be bride to the young Lochinvar."
The bride kissed the goblet; the knight took it up,
He quaffed off the wine, and he threw down the cup.
She looked down to blush, and she looked up to sigh,
With a smile on her lips and a tear in her eye.
He took her soft hand ere her mother could bar,—
"Now tread we a measure!" said young Lochinvar.

So stately his form, and so lovely her face,
That never a hall such a galliard did grace;
While her mother did fret, and her father did fume,
And the bridegroom stood dangling his bonnet and plume;
And the bride-maidens whispered, "Twere better by far
To have matched our fair cousin with young Lochinvar."

One touch to her hand and one word in her ear,
When they reached the hall-door, and the charger stood near;
So light to the croup the fair lady he swung,
So light to the saddle before her he sprung!
"She is won! we are gone, over bank, bush, and scaur;
They'll have fleet steeds that follow," quoth young Lochinvar.
There was mounting 'mong Graemes of the Netherby clan;
Forsters, Fenwicks, and Musgraves, they rode and they ran;
There was racing and chasing on Cannobie Lee,
But the lost bride of Netherby ne'er did they see.

So daring in love, and so dauntless in war,
Have ye e'er heard of gallant like young Lochinvar?

A Bird Came Down
by Emily Dickinson
A bird came down the walk:
He did not know I saw;
He bit an angle-worm in halves
And ate the fellow, raw.

And then he drank a dew
From a convenient grass,
And then hopped sidewise to the wall
To let a beetle pass.

He glanced with rapid eyes
That hurried all abroad,—
They looked like frightened beads, I thought;
He stirred his velvet head
Like one in danger; cautious,
I offered him a crumb,
And he unrolled his feathers
And rowed him softer home

Than oars divide the ocean,
Too silver for a seam,
Or butterflies, off banks of noon,
Leap, splashless, as they swim.

Daffodils
by William Wordsworth

I wander'd lonely as a cloud
That floats on high o'er vales and hills,
When all at once I saw a crowd,
A host, of golden daffodils;
Beside the lake, beneath the trees,
Fluttering and dancing in the breeze.

Continuous as the stars that shine
And twinkle on the Milky Way,
They stretch'd in never-ending line
Along the margin of a bay:
Ten thousand saw I at a glance,
Tossing their heads in sprightly dance.

The waves beside them danced; but they
Out-did the sparkling waves in glee:
A poet could not but be gay,
In such a jocund company:
I gazed—and gazed—but little thought
What wealth the show to me had brought:

For oft, when on my couch I lie
In vacant or in pensive mood,
They flash upon that inward eye
Which is the bliss of solitude;
And then my heart with pleasure fills,
And dances with the daffodils.

The Oak
by Alfred, Lord Tennyson

Live thy Life,
Young and old,

Like yon oak,
Bright in spring,
Living gold;

Summer-rich
Then; and then
Autumn-changed
Soberer-hued
Gold again.

All his leaves
Fall'n at length,
Look, he stands,
Trunk and bough
Naked strength.

Said the West Wind

by Isabella Valancy Crawford

I love old earth! Why should I lift my wings,
My misty wings, so high above her breast
That flowers would shake no perfumes from their hearts,
And waters breathe no whispers to the shores?
I love deep places builded high with woods,
Deep, dusk, fern-closed, and starred with nodding blooms,
Close watched by hills, green, garlanded and tall.
On hazy wings, all shot with mellow gold,
I float, I float thro' shadows clear as glass;
With perfumed feet I wander o'er the seas,
And touch white sails with gentle finger-tips;
I blow the faithless butterfly against
The rose-red thorn, and thus avenge the rose;
I whisper low amid the solemn boughs,
And stir a leaf where not my loudest sigh
Could move the emerald branches from their calm,—

Leaves, leaves, I love ye much, for ye and I
Do make sweet music over all the earth!

I dream by glassy ponds, and, lingering, kiss
The gold crowns of their lilies one by one,
As mothers kiss their babes who be asleep
On the clear gilding of their infant heads,
Lest if they kissed the dimple on the chin,
The rose flecks on the cheek or dewy lips,
The calm of sleep might feel the touch of love,
And so be lost. I steal before the rain,
The longed-for guest of summer; as his fringe
Of mist drifts slowly from the mountain peaks,
The flowers dance to my fairy pipe and fling
Rich odours on my wings, and voices cry,
"The dear West Wind is damp, and rich with scent;
We shall have fruits and yellow sheaves for this."

At night I play amidst the silver mists,
And chase them on soft feet until they climb
And dance their gilded plumes against the stars;
At dawn the last round primrose star I hide
By wafting o'er her some small fleck of cloud,
And ere it passes comes the broad, bold Sun
And blots her from the azure of the sky,
As later, toward his noon, he blots a drop
Of pollen-gilded dew from violet cup
Set bluely in the mosses of the wood.

When I Heard the Learn'd Astronomer
by Walt Whitman
When I heard the learn'd astronomer;
When the proofs, the figures, were ranged in columns before me;
When I was shown the charts and the diagrams, to add, divide, and

113

measure them;
When I, sitting, heard the astronomer, where he lectured with much
    applause in the lecture-room,
How soon, unaccountable, I became tired and sick;
Till rising and gliding out, I wander'd off by myself,
In the mystical moist night-air, and from time to time,
Look'd up in perfect silence at the stars.

A Laughing Song
by William Blake

When the green woods laugh with the voice of joy,
And the dimpling stream runs laughing by;
When the air does laugh with our merry wit,
And the green hill laughs with the noise of it;

When the meadows laugh with lively green,
And the grasshopper laughs in the merry scene;
When Mary and Susan and Emily,
With their sweet round mouths sing, "Ha ha he!"

When the painted birds laugh in the shade,
Where our table with cherries and nuts is spread:
Come live, and be merry, and join with me,
To sing the sweet chorus of "Ha ha he!"

To a Butterfly
by William Wordsworth

I've watched you now a full half-hour;
Self-poised upon that yellow flower
And, little Butterfly! Indeed
I know not if you sleep or feed.
How motionless!—not frozen seas
More motionless! And then
What joy awaits you, when the breeze

Hath found you out among the trees,
And calls you forth again!

This plot of orchard-ground is ours;
My trees they are, my Sister's flowers;
Here rest your wings when they are weary;
Here lodge as in a sanctuary!
Come often to us, fear no wrong;
Sit near us on the bough!
We'll talk of sunshine and of song,
And summer days, when we were young;
Sweet childish days, that were as long
As twenty days are now.

Robin Redbreast
by William Allingham
Good-bye, good-bye to Summer!
For Summer's nearly done;
The garden smiling faintly,
Cool breezes in the sun!
Our thrushes now are silent,—
Our swallows flown away, —
But Robin's here in coat of brown,
With ruddy breast-knot gay.
Robin, Robin Redbreast,
O Robin dear!
Robin singing sweetly
In the falling of the year.

Bright yellow, red, and orange,
The leaves come down in hosts;
The trees are Indian Princes,
But soon they'll turn to Ghosts;
The scanty pears and apples

Hang russet on the bough,
It's Autumn, Autumn, Autumn late,
'Twill soon be Winter now.
Robin, Robin Redbreast,
O Robin dear!
And welaway! my Robin,
For pinching times are near.
The fireside for the Cricket,
The wheatstack for the Mouse,
When trembling night-winds whistle
And moan all round the house;
The frosty ways like iron,
The branches plumed with snow,—
Alas! in Winter, dead and dark,
Where can poor Robin go?
Robin, Robin Redbreast,
O Robin dear!
And a crumb of bread for Robin,
His little heart to cheer.

Parenting

Proverbs 31:25–29
Strength and dignity are her clothing;
   And she laughs at the time to come.
She opens her mouth to wisdom;
   And the teaching of kindness is in her tongue.
She looks well to the ways of her household,
   And does not eat the bread of idleness;
Her children rise up and call her blessed,
   Her husband, also, and he praises her, saying
"Many women have done excellently,
   But you surpass them all."

Creativity

To Imagination
by Emily Jane Brontë

When weary with the long day's care,
And earthly change from pain to pain,
And lost, and ready to despair,
Thy kind voice calls me back again:
Oh, my true friend! I am not lone,
While then canst speak with such a tone!

So hopeless is the world without;
The world within I doubly prize;
Thy world, where guile, and hate, and doubt,
And cold suspicion never rise;
Where thou, and I, and Liberty,
Have undisputed sovereignty.

What matters it, that all around,
Danger, and guilt, and darkness lie,
If but within our bosom's bound
We hold a bright, untroubled sky,
Warm with ten thousand mingled rays
Of suns that know no winter days?

Reason, indeed, may oft complain
For Nature's sad reality,
And tell the suffering heart, how vain
Its cherished dreams must always be;
And Truth may rudely trample down
The flowers of Fancy, newly-blown:

But, thou art ever there, to bring
The hovering vision back, and breathe

New glories o'er the blighted spring,
And call a lovelier Life from Death,
And whisper, with a voice divine,
Of real worlds, as bright as thine.

I trust not to thy phantom bliss,
Yet, still, in evening's quiet hour,
With never-failing thankfulness,
I welcome thee, Benignant Power;
Sure solacer of human cares,
And sweeter hope, when hope despairs!

PROSE PASSAGES

Some passages of prose are like poetry, others like quotations. Reading one at a service can be a powerful way of illustrating the honoree's qualities and characteristics, especially if you are short on personal stories. Here are some examples of prose passages that could be incorporated into a ceremony.

Inspirational

The Power of Myth
by Joseph Campbell
People say that what we're all seeking is a meaning for life. I don't think that's what we're really seeking. I think what we're seeking is an experience of being alive, so that our life experiences on the purely physical plane will have resonance within our own innermost being and reality, so that we actually feel the rapture of being alive.

A Return to Love: Reflections on the Principles of a Course in Miracles
by Marianne Williamson
Our deepest fear is not that we are inadequate. Our deepest fear is that we are powerful beyond measure. It is our light, not our darkness that most

frightens us. We ask ourselves, Who am I to be brilliant, gorgeous, talented, fabulous? Actually, who are you *not* to be? You are a child of God. Your playing small does not serve the world. There's nothing enlightened about shrinking so that other people won't feel insecure around you. We are all meant to shine, as children do. We were born to make manifest the glory of God that is within us. It's not just in some of us; it's in everyone. And as we let our own light shine, we unconsciously give other people permission to do the same. As we are liberated from our own fear, our presence automatically liberates others.

Imaginative

George and Martha Round and Round
by James Marshall

George invited Martha
on an ocean cruise.
"Is *this* the boat?" said Martha.
"Use your imagination," said George.
"I'll try," said Martha.
Very soon it was raining cats and dogs.
"This is unpleasant," said Martha.
"Use your imagination," said George.
"Think of it as a thrilling storm
at sea."
"I'll try," said Martha.
"Lunch is served," said George.
And he gave Martha a soggy cracker. Martha was not impressed.
"Use your imagination," said George.
"Oh looky," said Martha. "What a pretty shark."
"A shark!" cried George. George took a spill. "But where's the shark?"
"Really," said Martha. "You must learn to use your imagination."

The Tempest
by William Shakespeare

Full fathom five thy father lies;
Of his bones are coral made;
Those are pearls that were his eyes:
Nothing of him that doth fade
But doth suffer a sea-change
Into something rich and strange.
Sea-nymphs hourly ring his knell:
Hark! now I hear them,—Ding-dong, bell.

House at Pooh Corner
by A. A. Milne

"Pooh, promise me you won't forget about me, ever. Not even when I am a
  hundred."
Pooh thought for a little.
"How old shall I be then?"
"Ninety-nine."
Pooh nodded. "I promise," he said.

House at Pooh Corner
by A. A. Milne

But wherever they go, and whatever happens to them on the way, in that
enchanted place on the top of the forest a little boy and his bear will always
be playing.

Oh, the Places You'll Go!
by Dr. Seuss

You'll be on your way up!
You'll be seeing great sights!
You'll join the high fliers
Who soar to high heights.

You won't lag behind, because you'll have the speed.
You'll pass the whole gang and you'll soon take the lead.
Wherever you fly, you'll be best of the best.
Wherever you go, you will top all the rest.

Our Town
by Thorton Wilder

We all know that *something* is eternal. And it ain't houses and it ain't names, and it ain't earth, and it ain't even the stars . . . everybody knows in their bones that *something* is eternal, and that something has to do with human beings. All the greatest people ever lived have been telling us that for five thousand years. . . . There's something way down deep that's eternal about every human being.

Friendship

George and Martha Encore
by James Marshall

Martha was so discouraged. Her garden was an ugly mess of weeds.
"I just don't seem to have a green thumb," she sobbed.
George hated to see Martha unhappy. He wanted so much to help. Suddenly George had a splendid idea. Very quietly George crept into Martha's garden and stuck tulips in the ground. But just then Martha happened to look out the window.
"Oh, dear," said George. "You're always catching me."
But Martha was so pleased.
"Dear George," she said. "I would much rather have a friend like you than all the gardens in the world."

Horton Hatches the Egg
by Dr. Seuss
I meant what I said
And I said what I meant
An elephant's faithful
One hundred percent.

Horton Hears a Who!
by Dr. Seuss
Should I put this speck down?..." Horton thought with alarm.
"If I do, these small persons may come to great harm.
I *can't*, put it down. And I *won't*! After all
A person's a person. No matter how small."

Nature

The Little Prince
by Antoine de Saint Exupéry
If someone loves a flower, of which just one single blossom grows in all the
millions and millions of stars, it is enough to make him happy just to look at
the stars. He can say to himself, "Somewhere, my flower is there".

Gardening

The Lorax
by Dr. Seuss
"So…
Catch!" calls the Once-ler.
He lets something fall.
"It's a Truffula Seed.

It's the last one of all!

You're in charge of the last of the Truffula Seeds.

And Truffula Trees are what everyone needs.

Plant a new Truffula. Treat it with care.

Give it clean water. And feed it fresh air.

Grow a forest. Protect it from axes that hack.

Then the Lorax

And all of his friends

May come back."

Free Spirit

The Tempest
by William Shakespeare
ARIEL
Where the bee sucks, there suck I.

In a cowslip's bell I lie;

There I couch when owls do cry.

On the bat's back I do fly

After summer merrily.

Merrily, merrily shall I live now

Under the blossom that hangs on the bough.

PROSPERO
Why, that's my dainty Ariel! I shall miss thee;

But yet thou shalt have freedom. So, so, so . . .

My Ariel, chick,

That is thy charge: then to the elements

Be free, and fare thou well!

Oh, The Places You'll Go!
by Dr. Seuss
You have brains in your head.

You have feet in your shoes.
You can steer yourself
Any direction you choose.
You're on your own. And you know what you know.
And YOU are the guy who'll decide where to go.

Yertel the Turtle
by Dr. Seuss
And today the great Yertle, that Marvelous he,
Is King of the Mud. That is all he can see.
And the turtles, of course...all the turtles are free
As turtles and, maybe, all creatures should be.

Wise

The Little Prince
by Antoine de Saint Exupéry
That is the most difficult thing of all. It is much more difficult to judge oneself than to judge others. If you succeed in judging yourself rightly, then you
are indeed a man of true wisdom.

Hamlet
by William Shakespeare
This above all: to thine own self be true,
And it must follow, as the night the day,
Thou cans't not be false to any man.

Our Town
by Thorton Wilder
Do any human beings ever realize life while they live it
—every, every minute?

As You Like It
by William Shakespeare
All the world's a stage,
And all the men and women merely players.
They have their exits and their entrances,
And one man in his time plays many parts,
His acts being seven ages.

Love

The Little Prince
by Antoine de Saint Exupéry
[The little prince] went back to meet the fox.
"Goodbye," he said.
"Goodbye," said the fox. "And now here is my secret, a very simple secret: It is only with the heart that one can see rightly; what is essential is invisible to the eye."
"What is essential is invisible to the eye," the little prince repeated, so that he would be sure to remember.
"It is the time you have wasted for your rose that makes your rose so important."
"It is the time I have wasted for my rose," said the little prince, so that he would be sure to remember.
"Men have forgotten this truth," said the fox. "But you must not forget it. You become responsible, forever, for what you have tamed. You are responsible for your rose . . ."
"I am responsible for my rose," the little prince repeated, so that he would be sure to remember.

Hamlet
by William Shakespeare
Now cracks a noble heart. Good night sweet prince:
And flights of angels sing thee to thy rest!

Song of Solomon 8:6–7

Set me as a seal upon thine heart,
    as a seal upon thine arm,
for love is as strong as death,
    jealousy as cruel as the grave.
Its flashes are flashes of fire,
    the very flame of the Lord.
Many waters cannot quench love,
    neither can the floods drown it.

1 Corinthians 13:1–13

What if I could speak all of humans and of angels? Without love, I would
    be nothing more than a noisy gong or a clanging cymbal.
What if I could prophesy and understand all secrets and all knowledge?
    And what if I had faith that moved mountains? I would be nothing
    without love.
What if I gave away all that I owned and let myself be burned alive? I
    would gain nothing, unless I loved.
Love is kind and patient; it is never jealous, boastful, or proud.
Love is never rude. Love is not selfish or quick tempered. It does not keep
    a record of wrongs that others do.
Love rejoices in the truth, but not in evil.
Love is always supportive, loyal, hopeful, and trusting.
Love never fails!
[. . .]
Now we see through a glass, darkly; but later we shall see God face to face:
    now I know only in part; but then shall I know even as I am known
    by God.
For now there are faith, hope, and love. But of these three, the greatest
    is love.

Philippians 1:3

Every time you cross my mind, I break out in exclamations of thanks
to God.

Song

8

Music That Matters

Whether you're planning a memorial service for a concert pianist, an opera buff, or someone who loved fifties rock-and-roll, music is an essential element of a personal, meaningful service. Like fingerprints, musical preferences are unique to each individual. Different types of music mark each phase of our lives. Listening to specific songs has the power to trigger a flood of memories. Obviously music is more important to some people than others, and the significance of music at services varies accordingly. But regardless of whether a service includes one song or ten, every musical piece should have relevance to the honoree.

THE ROLE OF MUSIC

Music often plays a therapeutic, comforting role for those attending a service. It unifies the community and gives everyone a way to participate. Songs invite guests to dip into nostalgia, contemplate the honoree's past, and remember their shared experiences.

When selecting musical pieces, you should be conscious of the mood each song will set. People tend to be reflective while sitting quietly waiting for the service to begin. One hopes that as the service progresses guests will gradually feel more at peace with the honoree's death. It is for this reason that traditionally music starts out soft and becomes increasingly more celebratory. The most striking example of this progression is the New Orleans Jazz funeral, which begins with a somber, dirge-like procession to the ceremony and concludes with a raucously joyful march to the reception.

Be sure to also consider which instruments will provide accompaniment for the service. There are many options available in addition to the more traditional organ or piano. You might consider chamber music, haunting flutes, an upbeat accordion, bagpipes, or even a marching band. Many musicians will perform for free for memorial services; you just have to ask.

Aside from singing, there are other ways that music can help people be part of the celebration. Clapping, finger bells or other hand instruments, humming, whistling, and chanting are all ways for everyone to contribute to the musical environment. You might also find that making a CD or playlist best suits your needs. If you can't fit all the songs you wish into the service, create a nostalgic musical backdrop for the reception.

MAKE A SERVICE MEANINGFUL WITH MUSIC

- Choose songs that best represent the honoree. Whether it is a country ballad or Chubby Checker's "Let's Do the Twist," use music that reflects the honoree's personality, values, or interests.

- If you would like people to sing along, have experienced singers lead the group and make sure both they and the accompanist have sheet music and know the songs.

- Don't feel you have to sing songs in their entirety. Choose two or three verses and make it clear that those are the only ones to be sung.

- When selecting a song, make sure you read all of the verses and only sing those that are appropriate. A lovely song like "The Water is Wide" is about heartbreak and abandonment, if you listen to the later verses.

- Make sure you understand the background of a song. Even "Ring Around the Roses" sounds innocent, but is actually about the plague in Europe during the fifteenth century.

- Playing prerecorded music as celebrants arrive or exit is perfectly acceptable.

- For someone who has expressed no musical preferences, you may still be able to find songs that speak to the person's character, personality, or name.

SONGS

The following songs have been categorized by theme to help you think about and select music for a memorial service.

RELIGIOUS

Title	Lyrics/Music	Performers
All Creatures of Our God and King (Paraphrase of "Canticle of the Brother Sun" by St. Francis of Assisi)	William H. Draper/ Unknown	James R. Lawson; The City of London Sinfonia with Wayne Marshall, Cambridge Singers
All Things Bright and Beautiful	Cecil F. Alexander/ Unknown	John Rutter with Michael O'Neal Singers, Marissa Woodall
Fairest Lord Jesus	Trans. by Joseph August Seiss/Unknown	Leontyne Price
For the Beauty of the Earth	Folliot S. Pierpoint/ Conrad Kocher	Eric Daub
He's Got the Whole World in His Hands	Unknown	Nina Simone, Perry Como, Laurie London
I Saw the Light	Hank Williams	Hank Williams
Jesus Walked That Lonesome Valley	Unknown	Elvis Presley, Jeanette Thompson
Joyful, Joyful We Adore Thee	Henry J. van Dyke/ Ludwig van Beethoven	Carlo Curley, Dan Miller
Let All Things Now Living	Katherine K. Davis/ Unknown	

Title	Lyrics/Music	Performers
Morning Has Broken	Eleanor Farjeon/ Unknown	Cat Stevens
Shall We Gather at the River	Robert Lowry	Bryn Terfel
Sheep May Safely Graze	J. S. Bach/Unknown	Mormon Tabernacle Choir
Swing Low, Sweet Chariot	Unknown	The Staple Singers
We Gather Together	Adrianus Valerius/ Theodore Baker	Thomas Kinkade
What a Friend We Have in Jesus	Joseph M. Scriven/ Charles C. Converse	Merle Haggard, Stanley Brothers
When Morning Gilds the Skies	Trans. by Edward Caswall/ Joseph Barnby	
Will the Circle Be Unbroken	Ada R. Habershon/ Charles H. Gabriel	Nitty Gritty Dirt Band

CLASSIC PROCESSIONALS

Title	Lyrics/Music	Performers
Amazing Grace	John Newton/Unknown	Johnny Cash, Ray Charles, Judy Collins, Jerry Garcia, Janis Joplin, Willie Nelson, Elvis Presley, Pete Seeger, Rod Stewart
Flee as a Bird	Mary S. B. Dana/ Unknown	Louis Armstrong
Majesty of the Blues	Wynton Marsalis	Wynton Marsalis
Nearer, My God, to Thee	Sarah Adams/ Lowell Mason	Elvis Presley, Mormon Tabernacle Choir

CLASSIC RECESSIONALS

Title	Lyrics/Music	Performers
I Shall Not Be Moved	Homer Morris	Johnny Cash, Mississippi John Hurt
Jesus Is on the Mainline	Unknown	Ry Cooder, Ben Harper
When the Saints Go Marching In	Unknown	Judy Garland, Elvis Presley, The Beatles

OPERA AND CLASSICAL

Title	Lyrics/Music	Performers
"Abends Will Ich Schlafen Gehn" from *Hänsel und Gretel*	Engelbert Humperdinck/ Adelheid Wette	Frederica von Stade, Judith Blegen
"Au Fond du Temple Saint" from *The Pearl Fishers*	Michael Carré/ Eugène Cormon, Georges Bizet	Roberto Alagna, Bryn Terfel
Ave Maria	Unknown/ Charles Gounod	Lisa Otto
Ave Verum Corpus	Unknown/ Wolfgang Mozart	Cambridge King's College Choir
Caro Mio Ben	Giuseppe Giordani	Cecilia Bartoli
Cradle Song	Karl Simrock/ Johannes Brahms	Celine Dion
"Ebben? Ne andrò lontana" from *La Wally*	Alfredo Catalani/ Luigi Illica	Wilhelmenia Wiggins Fernandez, Sarah Brightman
Going to Heaven	Emily Dickinson/ Aaron Copeland	Susan Chilcott, Iain Burnside
"Habanera" from *Carmen*	Henri Meilhac, Ludovic Halévy/ Georges Bizet	Maria Callas, Leontyne Price, Julia Migenes, Jessye Norman

Title	Lyrics/Music	Performers
"Hallelujah" from *Messiah*	Unknown/ George Frideric Handel	London Philharmonic Orchestra and Choir
"Je Crois Entendre Encore" from *The Pearl Fishers*	Eugène Cormon, Michael Carré/Georges Bizet	Roberto Alagna
"Mon Coeur S'Ouvre A Ta Voix" from *Samson et Dalila*	Ferdinand Lemaire/ Camille Saint-Saëns	Olga Borodina
"Nessun Dorma" from *Turandot*	Giuseppe Adami, Renato Simoni/ Giacomo Puccini	Luciano Pavarotti, Placido Domingo, Sarah Brightman
"O Mio Babbino Caro" from *Gianni Schicchi*	Giovacchino Forzano/ Giacomo Puccini	Kiri Te Kanawa
"O Soave Fanciulla" from *La Boheme*	Giovanni Capurro/ Eduardo di Capua	Luciano Pavarotti, Maria Freni
O Sole Mio	Luigi Illica, Giuseppe Giacosa/ Giacomo Puccini	Enrico Caruso, Mario Lanza, Luciano Pavarotti, Andrea Bocelli
"O Thou That Tellest Good Tidings to Zion" from *Messiah*	Charles Jennens/ George Frideric Handel	London Philharmonic Orchestra and Choir
"Quando M'En Vo' Soletta Per La Via" (Musetta's Waltz) from *La Boheme*	Luigi Illica, Giuseppe Giacosa/Giacomo Puccini	Kiri Te Kanawa
"Rejoice Greatly, O Daughter of Zion" from *Messiah*	Charles Jennens/ George Frideric Handel	London Philharmonic Orchestra and Choir
"Sous le Dôme Épais" (The Flower Duet) from *Lakme*	Edmond Gondinet, Philippe Gille/Léo Delibes	Joan Sutherland, Jane Berbie
"Un Bel Di Vedremo" from *Madama Butterfly*	Luigi Illica, Giuseppe Giacosa/Giacomo Puccini	Renata Scotto, Maria Callas, Kiri Te Kanawa

JAZZ

Title	Lyrics/Music	Performers
All the Things You Are	Oscar Hammerstein II/ Jerome Kern	Ella Fitzgerald, Frank Sinatra, Tony Bennett
And the Angels Sing	Johnny Mercer/ Ziggie Elman	Benny Goodman, Louis Armstrong
Come Rain or Come Shine	Johnny Mercer/ Harold Arlen	Ray Charles, Billie Holiday, Frank Sinatra
East of the Sun and West of the Moon	Brooks Bowman	Ella Fitzgerald, Sarah Vaughan, Frank Sinatra
Over the Rainbow	E.Y. Harburg/ Harold Arlen	Judy Garland, Ray Charles
Rhapsody in Blue	George Gershwin	Leonard Bernstein (piano/ conductor), New York Philharmonic Orchestra
Sophisticated Lady	Duke Ellington	Ella Fitzgerald
Stormy Weather	Harold Arlen/ Ted Koehler	Frank Sinatra
Stranger on the Shore	Robert Mellin/ Acker Bilk	Andy Williams, The Drifters, Benny Goodman, Acker Bilk
Summertime	DuBose Heyward, Dorothy Heyward, Ira Gershwin/ George Gershwin	Billie Holliday, Ella Fitzgerald, Louis Armstrong, Frank Sinatra, Janis Joplin

FOLK/TRADITIONAL

Title	Lyrics/Music	Performers
500 Miles	Hedy West	Joan Baez, Judy Collins
All My Trials	Unknown	Joan Baez

Title	Lyrics/Music	Performers
Down in the Valley	Unknown	Otis Redding
Drink to Me Only with Thine Eyes	Ben Johnson/ Unknown	Roy Clark, Paul Robeson
Every Night When the Sun Goes In	Unknown	Josephine Cameron, Gwyneth Walkeez
Forever Young	Bob Dylan	Bob Dylan
I Have a Million Nightingales	Mahmoud Darwish/ Linda Hirschhorn	Linda Hirschhorn
I'll Fly Away	Albert E. Brumley	Gillian Welch, Alison Krauss
Lord of the Dance	Elder Joseph Brackett/ Sydney Carter	Sydney Carter
The Ocean Refuses No River	Lila Flood	Lila Flood, Sydney Carter
Red River Valley	Unknown	Slim Whitman
Simple Gifts	Elder Joseph Brackett/ Unknown	Mary Ann Valaitis, Sabbathday Lake Shaker Community, Arthur Rawding, Robert Dobson, Boston Schola Cantorum, Boston Camerata
There Is So Much Magnificence	Peter Makena	Peter Makena
This Train	Unknown	Peter, Paul, and Mary
The Water Is Wide	Unknown	Eva Cassidy
Woyaya	Unknown	Art Garfunkel
You Are My Sunshine	Unknown	The Pine Ridge Boys, Bing Crosby, Gene Autry

COUNTRY/WESTERN

Title	Lyrics/Music	Performers
Angel Band	Unknown	Emmylou Harris
Angels	Nanci Griffith	Nanci Griffith
Angels Among Us	Alabama	Alabama
Breathe	Stephanie Bentley/ Holly Lamar	Faith Hill
Don't Fence Me In	Cole Porter, Robert Fletcher	Bing Crosby, Frankie Laine
Down to the River to Pray	Unknown	Alison Krauss
Home on the Range	Brewster Higley/ Daniel Kelley	Gene Autry, Pete Seeger
I Hope You Dance	Lee Ann Womack	Lee Ann Womack
Live Like You Were Dying	Tim McGraw	Tim McGraw
A Living Prayer	Alison Krauss and Union Station	Alison Krauss and Union Station
My Angel Is Here	Wynonna Judd	Wynonna Judd
Seeds	Pat Alger, Ralph Murphy	Kathy Mattea
Sending Me Angels	Jerry Lynn Williams, Frankie Miller	Kathy Mattea
There Is a Reason	Alison Krauss and Union Station	Alison Krauss and Union Station
Wayfaring Stranger	Unknown	Emmylou Harris
We'll Meet Again	Unknown	Rosemary Clooney
When You Say Nothing at All	Paul Overstreet/ Don Schlitz	Alison Krauss and Union Station
Your Long Journey	D. Watson/R. L. Watson	Emmylou Harris

SENTIMENTAL

Title	Lyrics/Music	Performers
Angel Flying Too Close to the Ground	Willie Nelson	Willie Nelson
The Best Is Yet to Come	Carolyn Leigh/ Cy Coleman	Frank Sinatra, Tony Bennett, Ella Fitzgerald
Blue Eyes Crying in the Rain	Fred Rose	Willie Nelson
Devoted to You	Felice and Boudleaux Bryant	Carly Simon, Everly Brothers, Linda Ronstadt
If Ever I Would Leave You	Alan Jay Lerner/ Frederick Loewe	Robert Goulet
I've Got My Love to Keep Me Warm	Irving Berlin	Rod Stewart, Billie Holiday, Ella Fitzgerald, Bette Midler
Jamaica Farewell	Irving Burgie	Harry Belafonte, Jimmy Buffett
Wind Beneath My Wings	Larry Henley/Jeff Silbar	Bette Midler, Judy Collins
You Don't Know Me	Cindy Walker/Eddy Arnold	Ray Charles, Elvis Presley, Harry Connick, Jr.
You Send Me	Sam Cooke	Tony Bennett, Rod Stewart, Chaka Khan
Young at Heart	Carolyn Leigh/ Johnny Richards	Frank Sinatra

MUSIC OF THE SIXTIES

Title	Lyrics/Music	Performers
A Whiter Shade of Pale	Keith Reid/Gary Brooker, Mathew Fischer	Procol Harum
Angel	Jimmy Hendrix	Jimmy Hendrix
Aquarius/Let the Sunshine In	James Rado, Gerome Ragni, Galt MacDermot	The Fifth Dimension
Both Sides Now	Joni Mitchell	Joni Mitchell
Bridge over Troubled Water	Paul Simon	Simon and Garfunkel
Dancing in the Street	Marvin Gaye, Ivy Hunter, William Stevenson	Martha and the Vandellas
Early Morning Rain	Gordon Lightfoot	Gordon Lightfoot, Grateful Dead, Eva Cassidy
In My Life	John Lennon, Paul McCartney	The Beatles, Judy Collins
Midnight Special	Unknown	Creedence Clearwater Revival, Odetta, Lead Belly
Reach Out (I'll Be There)	Lamont Dozier, Brian Holland, Edward Holland Jr.	The Four Tops
Save the Last Dance for Me	Doc Pomus, Mort Schuman	Drifters, Brook Benton, Harry Connick Jr.
(Sittin' on) The Dock of the Bay	Otis Redding/ Steve Cropper	Otis Redding
Stairway to Heaven	Jimmy Page, Robert Plant	Led Zeppelin
Yesterday	John Lennon, Paul McCartney	The Beatles

MUSIC OF THE SEVENTIES AND EIGHTIES

Title	Lyrics/Music	Performers
Fly Like an Eagle	Steve Miller	Steve Miller Band
My Sweet Lord	George Harrison	George Harrison
Respect	Otis Redding	Aretha Franklin
You Are So Beautiful	Billy Preston, Bruce Fisher	Joe Cocker, Al Green, Tanya Tucker, Diana Ross
You Are the Sunshine of My Life	Stevie Wonder	Stevie Wonder
You'll Accomp'ny Me	Bob Seger	Bob Seger and The Silver Bullet Band
You've Got a Friend	Carole King	Carole King

INSPIRATIONAL

Title	Lyrics/Music	Performers
Angel	Sarah McLaughlin	Sarah McLaughlin
Circle of Life	Elton John/Tim Rice	Elton John
Climb Every Mountain	Oscar Hammerstein II/ Richard Rogers	Tony Bennett, Kiri Te Kanawa
Cymbeline	William Shakespeare/ Loreena McKennitt	Loreena McKennitt
Dante's Prayer	Loreena McKennitt	Loreena McKennitt
The Impossible Dream (The Quest)	Joe Darion/Mitch Leigh	Richard Kiley
Love Is Everything	Jane Siberry	Jane Siberry, k.d. lang
Mummers Dance	Loreena McKennitt	Loreena McKennitt
The Rose	Amanda McBroom	Bette Midler

Title	Lyrics/Music	Performers
Sail Across the Water	Jane Siberry	Jane Siberry
Tears in Heaven	Eric Clapton	Eric Clapton
Who Knows Where the Time Goes?	Sandy Denny	Sandy Denny, Judy Collins, Eva Cassidy
You'll Never Walk Alone	Oscar Hammerstein II/ Richard Rogers	Louis Armstrong, Ray Charles, Judy Garland, Elvis Presley

REFLECTING INTERESTS OF THE HONOREE

Title	Lyrics/Music	Performers
Patriotism		
America the Beautiful	Katharine Lee Bates/ Samuel Ward	Ray Charles
Eternal Father, Strong to Save	Rev. William Whiting/ Rev. John B. Dykes	Mormon Tabernacle Choir
God Bless America	Irving Berlin	Kate Smith, Ray Charles
Marine's Hymn	Unknown/ Jacques Offenbach	Marine Corp Band, Mitch Miller
Gardening		
The Garden Song	David Mallett	Arlo Guthrie, Fran Friedman
Theatrical		
Art Is Calling for Me	Harry B. Smith/ Victor Herbert	Kiri Te Kanawa

FEATURING HONOREE'S NAME

Title	Lyrics/Music	Performers
Along Comes Mary	Tandyn Almer	The Association
Amanda	Boston	Boston
Danny Boy	Fred E. Weatherly/ Unknown	Harry Connick Jr., Carly Simon
Honeysuckle Rose	Fats Waller/ Andy Razaf	Ella Fitzgerald, Louis Armstrong
I Love You, Suzanne	Lou Reed	Lou Reed
Maria	Leonard Bernstein/ Stephen Sondheim	Richard Beymer
Mary Anne	Ray Charles	Ray Charles, Stevie Wonder
Sara	Jefferson Starship	Jefferson Starship
Sherry	Bob Gaudio	The Four Seasons
Suzanne	Leonard Cohen	Leonard Cohen
Sweet Caroline	Neil Diamond	Neil Diamond

SIGNIFICANT PLACES

Title	Lyric/Music	Performer
Alaska and Me	John Denver	John Denver
Arizona	Mark Lindsay	Mark Lindsay
Autumn in New York	Vernon Duke	Louis Armstrong, Ella Fitzgerald
Ballad of the Illinois Opry	REO Speedwagon	REO Speedwagon
Blue Hawaii	Leo Robin, Ralph Rainger	Elvis Presley

Title	Lyrics/Music	Performers
Blue Moon of Kentucky	Bill Monroe	Patsy Cline, Elvis Presley
California Dreamin'	John Phillips, Michelle Phillips	Mamas and Papas
Carolina in My Mind	James Taylor	James Taylor
Florida Room	Steely Dan	Steely Dan
Georgia on My Mind	Stuart Gorrell/ Hoagy Carmichael	Ray Charles, Willie Nelson, Louis Armstrong
God Blessed Texas	Alan Jackson	Alan Jackson
I Guess He'd Rather Be in Colorado	Taffy Nivert/Bill Danoff	John Denver
I Left My Heart in San Francisco	Douglas Cross/ George Cory	Frank Sinatra, Tony Bennett
Kansas City Blues	Charlie Parker	Janis Joplin
Kentucky	Everly Brothers	Everly Brothers
Kentucky Rain	Eddie Rabbit, Dick Heard	Elvis Presley
Massachusetts	The Bee Gees	The Bee Gees
Memphis, Tennessee	Chuck Berry	Chuck Berry, Elvis Presley, Rolling Stones
Midnight Train to Georgia	Jim Weatherly	Gladys Knight & the Pips
Montana	Frank Zappa	Frank Zappa
Moonlight in Vermont	John Blackburn, Karl Suessdorf	Ray Charles, Frank Sinatra, Ella Fitzgerald
My Old Kentucky Home	Stephen C. Foster	Hall Johnson Choir

Title	Lyric/Music	Performer
New York City Rhythm	Marty Panzer, Barry Manilow	Barry Manilow
New York, New York	Fred Ebb/John Kander	Frank Sinatra
New York State of Mind	Billy Joel	Billy Joel
North to Alaska	Johnny Horton	Johnny Horton
Ohio	Betty Comden, Adolph Green/ Leonard Bernstein	Kim Criswell, Audra McDonald
Oklahoma!	Oscar Hammerstein II/ Richard Rogers	Gordon MacRae, Hugh Jackman
Old Cape Cod	Claire Rothrock, Milton Yakus, Allan Jeffrey	Patti Page
Please Come to Boston	Dave Loggins	Kenny Chesney, Dave Loggins
Rainy Night in Georgia	Tony Joe White	Tony Joe White
Sands of Nevada	Mark Knopfler	Mark Knopfler
Song of Wyoming	John Denver	John Denver
Stop in Nevada	Billy Joel	Billy Joel
Sweet Home Alabama	Lynyrd Skynyrd	Lynyrd Skynyrd
The Tennessee Moon	Neil Diamond/ Dennis Morgan	Neil Diamond
Tennessee Waltz	Redd Stewart, Pee Wee King	Patti Page, Les Paul, Mary Ford
Texas Tornado	Tracy Lawrence	Tracy Lawrence

Title	Lyric/Music	Performer
When I Left East Virginia	Flatt and Scruggs	Flatt and Scruggs, Joan Baez
Wild Montana Skies	John Denver	John Denver

Symbolism

9
The Significance of Symbols

My friend Jane's mother spent her summers at a large lakefront property with a swimming pool that overlooked the water. Every day, weather permitting, she swam laps in the pool. Her bathing suit, an old-fashioned skirted suit in a loud piebald pattern, not unlike a brown spotted cow, hung on a hook at the entrance of the pool area for years. She would wear it with a white rubber bathing cap. It was also the swimsuit loaned to any female guest who arrived without one. For her seventy-fifth birthday, the young men in her family videotaped a humorous skit with one grandson wearing the outfit. She laughed uproariously along with the rest of her family. Everyone held such wonderful memories of her in this beloved bathing suit that it became a family icon.

When she died, her family went to the summerhouse to celebrate her life and say good-bye. As they were about to place the urn with her ashes in the ground at a corner of the property, one of the grandsons jumped up, disappeared, then returned with the bathing suit. They lovingly wrapped it around her urn before lowering it into the ground, a touching gesture that will live on in their memories. So strong is the symbol that whenever relatives see that brown mottled print they think of her and the strong loving force she played in their lives.

THE POWER OF SYMBOLS

Objects can evoke vivid memories of people—who they were, how they lived their lives—even if that object is an unassuming one. You might have a favorite hat, book, or pocketknife that reminds you of a special moment or a shared experience with someone. A physical object, music, or writing that reminds us of someone can be used as a symbol, and associating symbols with people who are gone can be very comforting.

Many of the symbols associated with memorial rituals in Western culture, while widely recognized and understood, can be impersonal. Flags flown at half-mast, weeping willows, and cemeteries full of carved headstones do little to help us grieve or celebrate the life of an individual.

On the contrary, as with the swimsuit example, symbols should be personal and uplifting, lending a deeper understanding of the honoree and perhaps even becoming a token that serves as a reminder after the service is over. Imagine handing out small keychain flashlights that everyone waves during the service to symbolize a shining path for the honoree. Using that light later will bring back memories. When selected with purpose, symbols can help glorify the moment, memorializing the honoree in a tangible way.

Displays

There are countless ways to display symbols. One of the most common is to arrange objects and photographs on a decorated table at the service or reception. Guests will welcome the chance to interact with the honoree's belongings. Make sure people are able to view the objects in a place where they can move freely, linger, and share stories.

Ensure that the objects are attractively displayed. Less is better than more—you don't want the table to look cluttered. Explore different lighting options for a more dramatic visual impact or secure the items in display cases. (This will also prevent them from getting lost.) If the relics are too worn or otherwise less attractive, they might not convey the image you want. You can use miniature replicas or something else to symbolize the actual objects, such as a cast metal toy tractor rather than a real one. If there is historical or personal significance to any of the objects, place a small card beside them explaining their importance. (While it is wonderful to be surrounded by the honoree's things, the memorial service is not the time to read the will or talk about how belongings are being divided.)

If you have one dramatic photograph that captures the honoree, consider having a large poster made and hang it in a prominent place. You might also consider accompanying your display with a digital slide show, video loop, or family movie.

Do not underestimate the importance of an attractive backdrop. For a more sophisticated look, drape a dark velvet cloth over the table before arranging your objects. To prop up papers, articles, or photographs, try creating three-legged easels out of heavy-gauge brass wire found at the hardware store.

TOKENS OF REMEMBRANCE

Consider giving friends and family a sentimental trinket that will keep the honoree in their thoughts long after the service. Tokens don't have to cost much; they just need to be well thought out. Here are a few examples.

Token	Significance
· Bell tied with ribbon	· Musical person; also symbolic of mourning
· Candle	· For an evening service or someone who loved romance, candlelight, or life
· Small foreign flags	· For a traveler or to represent honoree's homeland
· Flowers	· Honoree's favorite color, flower, or birth flower
· Hershey's Kisses	· Chocolate lover
· Packet of seeds	· To spread the memory of a person who loved gardening, flowers, nature, or ecology
· Shell	· Someone who loved the sea or island vacations

PROFESSIONS

Many professions have symbolic artifacts and tools of the trade. For someone in construction, a leather tool belt and tools are very emblematic. Similarly, a doctor's tools, such as a stethoscope and black bag, would evoke the caring nature of the profession. For a writer, a nicely displayed box of manuscripts and original handwritten notes could enhance a service. Similarly, displaying a photographer's pictures will tell a better story than simply talking about how the honoree was never without a camera. The key is to choose one thing and make sure it stands out. Hats, gloves, footwear, uniforms, badges, tools, equipment—all symbols of a person's profession—can add a very personal touch. Don't forget to lay out military service medals or other awards to further complete the portrait.

Many professions also have their own flag. Bright, bold, and eye-catching, flags representing military service, nautical flags, or even flags for clubs, associations, or countries of origin can be used to make an entranceway look distinguished (see References).

COATS OF ARMS AND FAMILY CRESTS

For a honoree who felt deeply connected to his or her ancestry, find out if the family has a crest or coat of arms. These dignified symbols bring a sense of pageantry to a service. Print them on cocktail napkins, in the program, or as banners.

HOBBIES

Celebrating a person's hobbies and interests, even those left behind due to age, practicality, or location, can paint a more complete picture of an honoree. For instance, who would have guessed the town accountant was the captain of his college football team? A number of symbols could help elucidate those early years: a football jersey or helmet, a college jacket, a yearbook, a school banner, or any other object that may trigger memories. They can be used as icons on the program, a photographic collage, or symbols decorating a cake—the possibilities are endless.

You can also highlight an honoree's involvement in societies or charitable organizations by displaying plaques, ribbons, awards, and relevant newspaper clippings. All of these items serve as wonderful reminders of the good the honoree has done.

For the gardener, a cluster of garden tools tied together with ribbons, or even a wheelbarrow filled with potted plants, evokes the memory of the honoree outside digging flowerbeds. For someone who loved bridge, a table scattered with playing cards would be a nice touch. A telescope for the amateur astronomer; rock climbing gear, a kayak, or paddles and life vest for the adventurer; musical instruments for the musician; brushes, a paint-smudged palette, and unfinished sketches for the artist—each one of these objects has the power to serve as a treasured reminder.

FLOWERS

It is no secret that flowers are a wonderful way to embellish and personalize a space. You can gather flowers in bunches, weave them into garlands, use them in a sculpture, create a trellis or archway with them, or use them to decorate a cake. You could ask guests to wear a specific flower or corsage. The local garden club might be a good resource for other creative ideas and planning advice.

When it comes to floral arrangement, don't be afraid to push some boundaries—even if the service is conventional in every other way. Brightly colored or unusual blooms are striking, upbeat, and celebratory—nothing like what most people associate with "sympathy" flowers. You can order a nontraditional bouquet by simply telling the florist what you do not want; for example, you can request no carnations, daisies, mums, or too many greens. These are often the less expensive fillers that tend to make every bouquet seem the same. If the honoree has a special connection to specific flowers, then make sure they have a strong presence in the arrangements and share their significance during the service.

For some, flowers may not have a place in the service or reception. There is nothing wrong with this. For instance, there may be more important artifacts that would be overshadowed by flowers. Think about using flowers in a way that is complementary and contextual to all of the other wishes and preferences of the honoree.

IN LIEU OF FLOWERS

More and more frequently, obituary notices request "charitable donations in lieu of flowers." This, however, does not mean that flowers will not have a place at the service. The family would simply rather see the money typically spent on sympathy bouquets put toward a cause the honoree felt passionate about. The next time you place a notice you may want to request the same.

SEASONAL FLORA

Often the hardest part about deciding what flowers to use and how to use them is the breadth of choices. If you are having trouble, consider using a frame of reference as a starting point. One obvious frame of reference is season—whether it is the season in which the service is being held, the honoree's favorite season, or a season that has a special meaning for family and friends. Also, if no particular flower has significance for the honoree, then you can choose seasonal blooms to create ambiance. The guests will associate those flowers, even if subliminally, with their memory of the event and the honoree. Each season has its own beautiful array of flowers and foliage.

BIRTH FLOWER

Incorporating a person's birth flower into a memorial service can be an easy, touching way to remember someone.

Month	Flower
January	Carnation
February	Violet
March	Daffodil
April	Sweet pea
May	Lily of the valley
June	Rose
July	Larkspur
August	Gladiolus
September	Aster
October	Marigold
November	Chrysanthemum
December	Poinsettia

Spring

The choices in springtime are fresh and delicate: daffodils, irises, lilies, pussy willows, and tulips—to name just a few. Dogwood, with each blossom marked by a cross and a red center, holds a special meaning for many. Orange blossoms, traditionally used for weddings, might also spark a fond association. Mixed bouquets or a single type of flower are both equally stunning. You can also use flowering tree branches or shrubs, such as forsythia and azaleas.

Summer

Summer provides a wealth of choices, such as sweet peas, roses, gladiolas, and poppies. You might consider picking one color as a theme and combining many different types of flowers in various shades. These monochromatic arrangements have become quite popular in the event planning industry.

Autumn

Autumn can present a challenge, but it also presents an opportunity to get creative. Pumpkins entwined with vines or baskets of multi-colored apples make festive décor as well as a delightful take-away for those attending the service. Indian corn, autumn leaves, or mums are also seasonal possibilities.

Winter

The obvious flower for winter is the poinsettia, which in abundance can create a rich backdrop. Baskets of oranges (alone or mixed with kumquats, tangerines, or even grapefruit) are colorful, fragrant, and lovely as a take-away. Winter also yields lush foliage. Evergreen branches, tied with colorful ribbon and accented with winterberries, are seasonal and beautiful. The traditional Yule log, made using white birch with candles, pine branches, and holly, also carries symbolism for many. Even an austere arrangement of bare branches makes a poignant statement.

Regional Flora

Another good frame of reference is location. Think about what is most memorable or appropriate for where you are holding the service or the honoree's hometown. For instance, if you are in New England and honoring someone from Dallas, you could create a southwestern-themed bouquet with birds of paradise, chili peppers, cactus, or yellow roses (the state flower of Texas).

Flower and Foliage Symbolism

Sometimes it helps to see how others interpret the symbolic meaning of objects, if only for inspiration. Here are some meanings commonly associated with flowers, with a focus on positive symbolism:

Plants	Associated Meanings
Apple blossom	Adventure, perseverance, hope
Azalea	Self-protecting, nurturing, ephemeral
Bamboo	Long life, enlightenment

Plants	Associated Meanings
Bird of paradise	Freedom
Carnation	Undying love, happiness
Cedar	Steadfast faith
Cypress	Hope
Daffodil	Cheerfulness, rebirth, chivalry
Daisy	Innocence, loyal love
Evergreens	Immortality
Fig	Prosperity
Gardenia	Love, joy, remembrance
Gladiolus	Remembrance
Grapes	Miracles, abundance
Hydrangea	Understanding
Iris	Wisdom, faith, valor
Ivy	Friendship, immortality
Larkspur	Swiftness
Laurel	Accomplishment, success
Lily	Purity
Lily of the valley	Return to happiness, complete life
Mums	Long life, compassion
Orchid	Refinement, perfection
Oak tree	Strength
Olive	Healing faith
Palm	Pilgrimage, rejoicing
Pansy	Remembrance, meditation
Pineapple	Hospitality
Poinsettia	Celebration, success
Pomegranate	Bounty, fertility, new life, immortality, unity
Poppy	Remembrance, eternal sleep
Queen Anne's lace	Sanctuary
Rose	Love, friendship, beauty
Rosemary	Fidelity, remembrance

Plants (continued)	Associated Meanings (continued)
Sage	Virtue
Shamrock	Irish heritage, luck
Snapdragon	Graciousness
Strawberry	Righteousness, humility
Sunflower	Foolish passion
Sweet pea	Good-bye, blissful pleasure
Thistle	Scottish heritage, defiance, remembrance
Tulip	Love
Wheat sheaves	Bountiful harvest, long life

Staging

"Staging" is the way you choose to present an arrangement, and it can extend far beyond the traditional vase or basket. Flowers are the perfect complement when creating a table display. A ski boot filled with pine and winterberries, a cowboy boot with thistles, or a running shoe with wildflowers are all easy pairings of flowers and artifacts. Place a vase on top of a pretty stack of books for a scholar or teacher. For a gardener, fill a galvanized watering can with loose stems of flowers. For someone who loved acting or ballet, consider a large bouquet of long-stem roses next to a pair of dance shoes. Each item reinforces the other and makes for a more personal display. You should also take lighting into account. If the arrangement is an important centerpiece, use a spotlight or prominent location to highlight the arrangement.

You do not have to pull off elaborate staging or floral arrangements by yourself. You can take your ideas to a florist or talented friend to make sure your arrangement will be both artistically and structurally sound. The right florist will greet your suggestions with enthusiasm for the opportunity to do something out of the ordinary. If you don't know anything about the names or characteristics of flowers, bring pictures of flowers or other arrangements you find pleasing. If you have access to a completed Personal Portrait and Wishes Profile, you could take it to your florist and create a personal arrangement from that information.

BELOVED PETS

When an animal lover leaves a treasured pet behind, think about whether it would be appropriate to include animals in the service. If dogs were an honoree's passion, then bringing pets to the service would be a wonderful reminder of the honoree's characteristic love and kindness. If an honoree was part of a large circle of dog owners, consider having a service where all can bring their dogs. A fishbowl for someone who loved fish or fishing, or birds in cages for an avid bird watcher, are other examples of how to incorporate animals into a service. If certain pets are too difficult to handle (be sure to have someone at the service to tend to the animals), not welcome by some guests, or for some other reason unable to attend, display pictures of the pets so they are symbolically present.

FRAGRANCE

The sense of smell is a frequently forgotten sense, but it is a very powerful one. Fragrances can help us recall memories and make associations.

If the honoree always wore a particular perfume, you could use it to subtly scent the programs—just as women used to do with their letters. Simply place one drop of the perfume on each of the programs and leave in a box overnight. A favorite scarf lightly scented with perfume and draped on an easel displaying pictures, or tied to the handle of a basket containing non-fragrant flowers, can also evoke comforting memories. If you are holding the service in a space with a kitchen nearby and a traditional family dish is baking in the oven, there is no need to add any additional aromas.

Many natural fragrances are believed to have healing properties. For instance, the scent of lavender is known for its relaxing, soothing effects. You might find that your local nursery is willing to loan you pots of lavender for the day of the service. Or, you could incorporate the uplifting, energizing scents of lemon, peppermint, or rosemary.

If you are going to use fragrance, use it in moderation. Scent can easily become overpowering, even nauseating, and conflicting scents are downright unpleasant. Even heavily scented flowers such as lilies can become overwhelming in a closed room. Scented candles and other artificial scents should also be avoided. A gentle, natural fragrance is your safest option.

COLOR

Who do you think of when you see the color yellow, or lime green, or turquoise? By exploring what colors you associate with an honoree, you will discover meaningful ways to embellish the service. Perhaps you associate a specific color with the honoree because it was the color he or she loved to wear. Or perhaps it is a color linked to one of the honoree's most notable belongings, such as an automobile or a brown-spotted swimsuit.

Tying votives with a certain color ribbon, picking flowers of a specific color, releasing colored balloons scripted with heartfelt messages—there are a number of ways to symbolically use color. If a color had a specific meaning or association for the honoree, use that same association at the memorial service. And forget about color theory; there is no right or wrong interpretation.

THOUGHTS ON BLACK

It is my feeling that, unless there is a significant link with the honoree, black should be avoided. If your intention for the memorial service is to celebrate the honoree's life, black is a gloomy choice. However, for those occasions when black is the most appropriate color, consider combining it with white or another color so that the overall effect is a little brighter.

10
Tradition

Throughout the ages, people have established unique, beautiful ways to honor the dead and bring closure to the living. Exploring these cultural and spiritual practices can offer you a wealth of inspiration when planning a memorial service. With a little creativity, many of these rituals can easily be adapted for a modern-day ceremony.

The point is not to stage elaborate, historically accurate mourning rituals. Any ideas that you pull from another culture or time period should have relevance to the honoree. The ritual should be comforting and offer an enriching experience for friends and family. If the ritual does not meet those criteria, it does not belong at the service. Be selective, and focus primarily on cultures, regions, and religious traditions that have a direct connection to the honoree.

AFRICAN TRADITIONS

In some African cultures, the family collects a handful of earth covering the grave and places it in a ceremonial jar. In a "bringing-home" procession, they carry the ceremonial jar and put it in a place of honor, then invite the community to a night vigil honoring the loved one's memory. This simple, community-building tradition is adaptable for a modern procession with or without a night vigil.

The Akan of Ghana make an earthen pot, called an *abusua kuruwa*, which friends and family fill with tokens and mementos symbolic of life and rebirth. A potter friend might take pride in making a custom bowl for the occasion; although a large bowl, vase, or chest will work equally well.

To incorporate this idea into a memorial service, ask friends to bring with them positive symbols of life and rebirth, such as pictures, stuffed animals, ceramic statues, porcelain eggs, light green ribbon, flowers, or poems about spring. Collect the objects either during the service or afterwards and place them in a vessel of your choice.

In the Fon tradition (from the Republic of Benin), great metal altars called *asens* are constructed from tall iron poles. These poles hold a flat metal disk adorned with metal sculptures and decorations, usually of people, animals, and objects symbolic of the family and representative of the life that the honoree led.

NEW ORLEANS JAZZ FUNERAL

One of the most outstanding models for how music contributes to a memorial celebration is the New Orleans jazz funeral. This unique tradition is based on the African belief that death is not the end of life, but rather a joyous transition into the peaceful spirit realm. The music and participation of mourners in the ceremony clearly reflects that belief.

The ceremony follows a set of time-honored traditions. Family and friends begin the procession by walking from the honoree's home to the cemetery. A full jazz band, comprised of saxophones, trumpets, trombones, clarinets, and drums, accompanies the family along their journey and plays slow and somber dirges such as "Amazing Grace," "Flee As a Bird," and "Nearer My God To Thee." These hymns of sorrow and loss help the family mourn their loved one's passing, and give them a medium to express the intensity of their emotions.

During the procession, the core group of family, friends, and musicians makes up the "main line." This group leads the parade along its route to the cemetery, and then afterwards heads the pageant in a joyful march through the streets and eventually to the reception. Drawn by the fine music and good company, members of the community and bystanders often accompany the main line and make up the procession's "second line." In jazz funerals, these "second-liners" are known for their vibrant costumes, raucous singing, and jubilant dancing.

As the procession reaches the cemetery, the bandleader silences the musicians, and all pay proper respect while the honoree is laid to rest. When the funeral service is over, the band strikes up again, but this time the music is jubilant. This musical celebration is called "cutting the body loose," and prepares the honoree's spirit for its journey to the afterlife. The band plays raucous renditions of "When the Saints Go Marching In," "Didn't He Ramble," "I Shall Not Be Moved," and "Jesus Is on the Mainline" as the procession leaves the cemetery.

As the parade makes its way through the streets, members often stop along the way to visit with friends, enjoy refreshments and, most importantly, change their clothes. Family and friends shed their somber, black funeral attire and don colorful, festive garb more in line with the joyous nature of the procession. Men in the main line dress in richly colored hats and suits (pink, red, and white being the colors of choice), while women adorn themselves in sequined dresses, feathered fans, leather boots, silk hats, lace gloves, velvet sashes, linen handkerchiefs, and lacy parasols, all in the brightest of hues. This happy attire is worn in jubilation and celebration of the honoree and the eternal happiness of the hereafter.

The New Orleans jazz funeral provides a unique and inspirational way to commemorate a loved one's legacy, celebrating their life through procession, spectacle, dancing, and music.

ALASKAN ART

Many tribes of British Columbia and Southeast Alaska carve totem poles with the emblems and sacred animals that were important to the deceased. Figures on the totem poles are representative of the special events that occurred throughout a lifetime.

For the explorer or a person of native Alaskan descent, consider displaying wood carvings, prints, slides, or posters of distinctive Alaskan art. Create a makeshift totem pole from found objects that reflect the history, life, or interests of the honoree. Another option could be wrapping a telephone pole leading into the memorial service with colorful posters or creating a stand-up cylinder display at the reception.

CELTIC CUSTOMS

The Celtic people of the British Isles used to ignite the area around their loved one's bier, which they topped with personal items such as jewelry, armor, or trade tools. The community would gather for a feast, sing traditional mourning songs, and stage competitions in pole vaulting, high jumping, and darts.

To bring this Celtic tradition into a modern setting, display a large photograph of the honoree on an easel at the service. Encourage guests to bring an object that reminds them of the honoree; arrange the objects around the easel and encircle the small memorial with lit candles. Play favorite songs and intersperse the music with storytelling and readings. For the reception, plan an outdoor picnic with a few organized outdoor games.

CHINESE WATER LANTERNS

The Ghost Festival is a special holiday when the Chinese pay homage and offer thanks to their ancestors. A time of great celebration and feasting, this ancient tradition usually falls in mid-to late August. As part of the festivities, Chinese lanterns, formed in the shape of lotus flowers, are set atop a buoyant piece of wood and cast upon the water. The lit candles dancing on the water's surface is a remarkable sight.

You can buy biodegradable water lanterns or you can make your own. There are a number of creative ways to incorporate them into a service and the act of lighting them or casting them into a body of water offers guests a wonderful opportunity to participate in the ceremony.

THE DAY OF THE DEAD

The Day of the Dead is a traditional Mexican holiday held on November 1st and 2nd (All Saints' Day and All Souls' Day). Intended as a time for rejoicing and celebrating the lives of deceased loved ones, both days are filled with elaborate traditions of festivities, food, and prayer. Mexicans in cities around the world celebrate this holiday, and there are variations in Spain as well.

You can mark this holiday as a day of remembrance or use it as the theme for a memorial service. For your own ceremony, erect an altar with a lighted candle surrounded by marigolds. Decorate the altar with the honoree's portrait; a spread of fruit, meat, and bread; and a sentimental selection of the honoree's former belongings. Sprinkle flower petals along the path to the front door. The traditional foods of The Day of the Dead are *pan de muerto*, a traditional bread in the shape of a skull and crossbones, and *atole*, a sweet drink made of fruit and corn. Both are relatively easy to make.

FUNERAL BELLS

From ancient times and until quite recently, tolling the bell was the customary way to signal the death of a loved one. Both the number of tolls and their pitch relayed information about the deceased, such as their age, station, and gender. You can ring bells at any time before, during, or after the service. Traditionally, the bell rings twice for a woman, three times for a man, and four or more times for a member of the clergy. After a pause, the bell tolls for the number of years the person lived. Bells rung at the end of the service should be in jubilation, celebrating the life the person led and rejoicing in the happiness the honoree will experience in the afterlife.

If you decide to ring funeral bells at a memorial service, you might consider including a brief paragraph in the back of the program explaining the historical significance of funeral bells and what the different rings mean.

FUNERAL BISCUITS

Funeral biscuits are a lost tradition, brought to America by early British settlers. From the seventeenth through nineteenth centuries, funeral biscuits were so prevalent at funerals that mentioning their presence would be akin to mentioning the casket or the gravestone. It was simply assumed that funeral biscuits would be served. Similar to Scottish shortbread and their modern-day counterparts, ladyfingers, these little rectangular biscuits were made of wheat flour, eggs, sugar, and caraway seeds. They were stamped with a personal symbols, such as an initial, a heart, winged cherub, or the fleur-de-lis. Once baked, the biscuits were wrapped in white paper and inscribed on the inside with phrases commemorating the soul's passage to the eternal realm.

The recipe used for funeral biscuits varies widely both culturally and regionally. Use your favorite shortbread, sugar cookie, or springerle recipe—one with firm dough that will hold its shape once stamped and baked. Eliminate all other flavorings in the recipe and add approximately one teaspoon of caraway seeds for each cup of flour during the final mixing. Pat or roll the dough into the thickness your recipe calls for, ideally one-third to one-half inch. Use a cookie press, wooden embossing roller, or individual stamp purchased from your local craft store to press a symbol into the raw dough. Bake according to your recipe's directions and cut into rectangles or in a shape that conforms to your stamp. When cool, wrap cookies individually in white parchment paper. If you decide to forgo the traditional funeral biscuit, consider serving the honoree's favorite cookie instead.

ANCIENT GREEKS

The ancient Greeks believed that honoring the dead was as important as caring for the living. The body of the deceased was washed in seawater, wrapped in a white shroud, and laid out on a bed with an elaborately decorated bier cloth. To show their respect, mourners would place a crown on the honoree's head and a silver coin on his or her lips. The first phase of the funeral was the ritual lamenting by friends and relatives, and often a heartbreakingly beautiful ode was sung in the honoree's memory.

At your own service, display a beautiful scarf or fabric sprinkled with shiny coins around a ceremonial hat, such as a military beret. Display or serve pomegranates, which symbolize rebirth in Greek mythology. Or, use pomegranate juice in a beverage or punch and provide guests with a brief explanation of the fruit's meaning.

NATIVE AMERICANS

The great Chief Seattle once said, "There is no death, only a change in worlds." For the tribes of North America and the First Nations of Canada, death was experienced not as an end, but as a passage to another realm, free of suffering and hardship. Their customs recognized that the deceased was beginning the next phase in the cycle of existence and needed a proper and respectful farewell for embarking upon the journey.

The Lakota crafted "spirit bundles" by wrapping a lock of the honoree's hair in holy cloths. The women of the family sewed special clothing for the deceased, symbolic of the new form to be assumed in the afterlife. A tribal elder would paint a portrait of the honoree onto a round board and attach it to a pole measuring the same height as the honoree. Finally, the medicine man of the tribe would come forward and perform a ritual releasing the loved one's spirit, sending it on its journey down Spirit Road.

There are many published Native American blessings and prayers. These could be included in a memorial service for someone who respected nature, the land, or simply possessed a deep appreciation for the different cultures of the Native Americans.

SACRED STONES

During Europe's Bronze Age, prehistoric people erected elaborate stone burial monuments, called cairns, from thousands of small rocks to mark grave sites. On the other side of the world in Asia, pilgrims traveling from far and wide would bring a small stone from their hometown or from a place along their journey and lay it in the temple yard of a pagoda, as a prayer stone for the Buddha. Over the centuries these small stones have accumulated into lovely stone gardens. Similar commemorative cairn traditions are found in Native American culture.

Create your own stone tribute by holding a simple ceremony where each person brings a small rock to create a cairn in a place once frequented by the honoree. A more elaborate stone sculpture would also provide a lasting memorial and a place for loved ones to grieve, especially if the honoree's ashes were scattered or the body was buried in a location inaccessible to friends and family.

SIGNALING AT SEA

Since the beginning of maritime history, seafarers have used visual systems of communication including flags, lanterns, and flares to convey important messages at sea. Like so many maritime traditions, signaling at sea is steeped in history and custom, and carries both a symbolic and practical purpose. Pennants, Semaphore flags, and signal lights are forms of communication that have won battles, saved lives, and inspired the imaginations of countless generations.

Colorful marine flags strung across the entranceway to a service will create a striking focal point for someone whose traditions or hobbies were connected with the water. In a darkened church, using Morse code and signal lanterns to spell the person's name or send a final message can be very poignant. This is especially true for men and women who served the country in wartime. In a seaside service, shoot flares into the sky as a welcoming or departing gesture.

WAKES AND VIGILS

Holding a wake or a vigil is one of the simplest, yet most expressive, ways to remember someone who has died. From the solemn remembrance of sitting shivah to the raucous gaiety of an Irish wake, cultures throughout history have developed traditions that help ease the pain of loss.

Buddhist Vigil

Buddhists in the small Himalayan country of Nepal have a ceremony that could easily be reenacted in a Western setting. In a three-day vigil, they burn incense, sound chimes and prayer horns, chant prayers, and sing hymns to the deceased's soul, giving it comfort and guidance for the journey into the next world. They make a small paper flag, inscribe it with the honoree's name, and place it in the center of a platform containing 108 votive candles. The entire family gathers around this table, and one by one, light each candle until the platform glows brilliantly. Attendees sing hymns and chant prayers for three days, and at the end of the third day, they light the flag to signify the release of the honoree's spirit into the afterlife, thus concluding the vigil.

Irish Wake

One of the most well-known funeral traditions in Western culture is that of the Irish wake. Since the time of the Celts, the people of Ireland and Scotland have held rowdy and boisterous vigils in honor of their deceased loved ones. Many people who have attended an Irish wake describe it as an incredibly cathartic experience. They are allowed to speak candidly about their emotions surrounding their loss and are encircled by a community united in grief, joy, rage, sorrow, and all the varied and spontaneous emotions that emerge when a loved one dies.

Sitting Shivah

On the other end of the spectrum is the somber Jewish mourning tradition of sitting shivah. This seven-day period of grief usually takes place in the honoree's house, or at the home of the person most directly affected by the loss. They light a memorial candle that burns for the entire period and represents the immortal soul of the honoree. The immediate family participates in the vigil, although other mourners are also welcome to attend.

They gather in the living room and sit on low cushions or on the floor to show that they have been humbled by their grief. The first meal of shivah is called the *seudat havra'ah*, the meal of consolation, which traditionally consists of lentils, hard-boiled eggs, and round bread. Their round shapes recall the cyclical nature of life. During the period of shivah, mourners from the community arrive to give their condolences to the family. They clean their hands at the basin left outside the entryway, alternately washing each hand three times to rinse away the sadness of death and focus on the life-giving powers of the water. They enter the house silently, and sit amongst the family, often saying nothing, just sharing in the family's loss. Mourners often bring small gifts, such as candies. It is also traditional to give a *tzedakah*, a charitable contribution, to the deceased's designated charity or organization.

Every day, mourners gather together to form a minyan, a quorum of ten adults, so the family can recite the daily kaddish prayer for the deceased. At the end of the seven days of mourning, the family and any mourners present conclude the shivah by leaving the shivah house and taking a walk around the block.

11

Second Chances

Sometimes there is simply no time to plan. When my brother died unexpectedly, arrangements for his funeral were made within a week. We soon realized that the shock of his death and the hurried circumstances of the event did not offer his loved ones adequate time to celebrate his life. It became so clear to me that we needed a second chance. So, a few months later, my family planned a weekend-long destination memorial service and took the time to honor, remember, and celebrate my brother. Our time together was moving, beautiful and, unlike the first funeral service, it was fun. Honoring him in this way gave us all a sense of completion and peace.

A SECOND SERVICE

There are many opportunities to hold a second memorial celebration. You can choose an anniversary, birthday, special holiday, a date when more people will be able to attend, or simply a season with more favorable weather. Oftentimes the second celebration, because time has passed, will be more celebratory and not as difficult as the first, more immediate ceremony. A second service does not need to be more inclusive; in fact, it might be that the family would appreciate something that brings them together in a more intimate way than a public event. However you say good-bye, whether it is a first, second, or third time, you should never have regrets.

When you know that people will not be able to gather immediately, then you should plan for a second service. Even if you don't have an exact date, letting people know they can expect something later on can be a relief, especially for people who would like to participate but cannot on short notice. Planning a memorial service and reception that takes place weeks, if not months, later will give you time to ensure people who want to participate can. Waiting for appropriate weather is also perfectly acceptable; for example, if there is to be a scattering of ashes around a favorite landscape, the ground should be soft.

One of the most difficult aspects of making arrangements is planning across long distances. It is becoming more and more common for relatives to move away from one another. Retired people may have a winter home but a different summer home, developing close friendships in both places. When relatives and friends are located in disparate locations, consider holding two services to accommodate both groups. Trying to remotely plan something memorable in an environment you are not familiar with is difficult and can take additional time. Whatever the circumstances, allow yourself adequate time to do it right. Sometimes that will mean doing it twice.

LIVING LEGACY

Even if the first memorial service was everything everyone needed to feel they had celebrated the honoree, you may still want the honoree to be remembered beyond the memorial service. For the doctor whose story was told earlier, it made sense to hold a local service for close family and colleagues followed by a symposium months later that gathered his medical colleagues. In addition, it also built a living legacy. Students for years to come will benefit from the scholarship funded by the symposium in the doctor's honor.

You do not have to be famous, rich, or have a lot of clout to create a meaningful living legacy. The idea is to find something within your price range that embodies the honoree's memory, connecting him or her with something that was important and can continue to benefit others. The following are some ways to continue celebrating an honoree.

Scholarships

There are many different kinds of scholarships—you're limited only by your imagination. With a scholarship, the donor's contribution and the recipient both receive recognition. Even the smallest scholarships are meaningful. Specifying the area of study such as nursing, art, or another field that mirrors an interest of the honoree will make the fund even more personal.

Camp

Consider a scholarship for a camp that has ties in some way to the honoree, such as 4-H, drama, or athletics.

Conference

Perhaps the honoree supported a professional conference; consider establishing a scholarship for someone in a related graduate program.

Concert

If music was the honoree's passion, donate a set of concert tickets each year to a group of deserving students.

Memorial Plaque

Memorial plaques are everywhere—public gardens, churches, hospitals, museums, universities; the list goes on. Some are large and represent large amounts of money. Others require just a small contribution or none at all. Buying a book inscribed with the honoree's name for a library or giving a donation to order books are both thoughtful ways of honoring someone's memory.

Star Naming

In Greek mythology, constellations and stars were named to immortalize both earthly and divine figures. In many relationships it is difficult to imagine the life of one without the other—true love, soul mates, fatherhood, motherhood, brotherhood, sisterhood. To commemorate these kinds of deep, sustaining relationships, consider naming stars after the honoree and that one you could not imagine the honoree without. Naming a star would also commemorate anyone who loved astronomy, astrology, or simply appreciated gazing up at a starry sky.

There are many organizations that sell star naming rights. None of them have any authority to do so except the International Astronomical Union (IAU). Their goal is to make all stars identifiable and recorded for scientific purposes; so they use numbers, not names. The only stars with official names are those established long ago by mythology and early astronomers.

You will find many organizations online that offer to register your star for a fee. Be aware that any promise for ownership of any kind has no legal basis. You can use a registry if you want the simplicity of having another organization help you identify the star and the star's location. Some send an official-looking certificate, pictures, and instructions for locating the star in the sky. Naming a star is a symbolic act so it doesn't have to be official.

You do not have to spend any money to name a star after an honoree. Instead, go to the library and ask for a book with star charts. Pick a constellation that has meaning, for some personal reason such as the mythological story behind it, its name, or the astrological month. Find a star within the constellation that does not have a number assigned by the IAU and designate that star for the honoree. At the memorial service, you can share with everyone which star you have selected for the honoree and show them all how to find it.

Public Event

Hosting a walk, bike ride, or marathon to raise money for a charity in the honoree's names is becoming more and more common. Another trend is holding charitable sporting events, such as a soccer, softball, or basketball game. Sometimes celebrity athletes will even participate in these kinds of events.

Also consider hosting a charitable event such as a pond, trail, or park clean-up day, or working in a soup kitchen or nursing home. Charity auctions and golf tournaments are other ways to raise money in memory of an honoree's passion.

Food or Drink

There is a private club in New York with a wonderful collection of sterling silver cups, each inscribed with a departed member's name. The cups are a timeless reminder of the members who have gone before. If you order the club's signature drink, a "Silver Cup," you will be toasting a particular late member as you lift your cup.

For a regular customer, a restaurant may consider renaming a sandwich, burger, or drink after an honoree.

Gifts

Is there something the honoree's favorite organization needs? Whether you fund a small repair, refurbish or replace aging equipment, or buy a new flag, there is satisfaction in knowing that the honoree's presence will be felt and acknowledged. It doesn't need to be something expensive; the most welcome items are not always the ones that cost the most. If you aren't sure what is needed, ask beforehand so the gift will be appreciated.

You could also purchase something for a charity auction in the honoree's name. It doesn't have to be a cruise; it can be as simple as a bottle of his or her favorite wine or something the honoree traditionally provided for the event.

Website

More and more people are creating memorial websites. Hosted for free, the site will truly be a living legacy, one that is always changing and reflecting the honoree through the words of family and friends. Create a site that only allows approved content to be posted to protect the legacy of your loved ones. Be sure there are no vindictive posts, and the honoree is portrayed in a positive light.

Remembering

The traditional times to remember honorees are on holidays and anniversaries. Planting flowers on the gravesite, saying a prayer at the dinner table, or sending an annual charitable donation are all simple ways to acknowledge the honoree is missed. As a family, you can create traditions that keep a memory alive.

12

Seven Surreptitious
Ways to Plan

When my friend Hope died, no one gathered at her local church. Instead, we were invited to an evening gala for dinner and dancing at her favorite art museum. Everyone dressed in formal party attire, toasts were made, and the mood was effervescent. Because Hope loved to dance and host a good party for her friends, that is how she chose to be remembered. She had planned ahead and her loved ones knew how best to celebrate her life. This extravagant event was a true reflection of Hope's personality and style.

No one likes to think about death. We prefer to think about living. Even though we know we should plan for the inevitable, the predictable questions always arise: How do I talk about this? How do I convey my wishes?

There are many surreptitious ways for you to plan. Not in a covert way, but rather with style and substance that will save you time and heartache later. Planning in the moment can be so difficult; so much is overlooked. Many of the ideas presented here will help you look at planning a memorial in new ways. The goal is to plan without dread and foreboding, in a way that can be enlightening and even entertaining. It will most certainly lighten the load when the moment comes and ensure that you and your loved ones are properly remembered. Starting with a general idea and knowing what specific information you need to plan a memorable event will make the entire process easier.

One of the most helpful things you can do to plan for your loved ones is broaching the subject at a neutral time. When someone comments on a memorial service, ask what that person would do the same or differently, what parts they liked and disliked. Oftentimes the subject will be dismissed or the conversation stopped; most people want to "talk about it later." Instead, try to encourage the discussion when the opportunity arises. If someone mentions a favorite thing such as a kind of food, poem, or song and you think it might be appropriate for a service, ask if it is something the person deeply identifies with or would like to be remembered for liking. Rather than trying to make connections completely out of context, ask when someone offers a suggestion or appears ready to talk. The key to planning is being aware.

Often the same information you need for a memorial service can be found in other life moments. While reading about the different approaches and ways to plan in this chapter, think about gatherings and events in your life that you can use to strategize for your own service and for those close to you.

IDEA 1: THE PLANNING PARTY

In my circle of friends, we throw annual parties that have become traditional events for our group. Someone holds a winter solstice party, or the first summer barbeque. I always hold a Boxing Day party. What if, instead of turning to social banter during a party, you instead talk about your ideas for planning a memorial service? Even if you are only forty and think it is too early to plan, you might find that thinking about how you want to be remembered will help you think about how you want to live. Have you achieved your goals, accomplished all you can, made the contributions to society you imagine as your legacy? When people describe you, do they characterize you in the same way you see yourself? While it is trite to say you can't start planning too soon, there is value in recording information and reviewing how your wishes change over the years. A party with this focus can easily become part of your group's social traditions.

Think about the times you get together with friends in a relaxed environment. Perhaps you have a hiking group, or maybe a dinner group. In the evening, after a day's hike or after a group dinner, might be a perfect time to try constructing your memorial service portraits. If you want to clue people in ahead of time, you can send out the Personal Portrait and Wishes Profile (see pages 27-29) beforehand and ask everyone to be prepared to fill it out. Having a party with your closest friends, relatives, club members, or even people you don't know very well can make planning fun. It can be an opportunity to think about how you want to be remembered while finding out how others view you and your achievements. You might be surprised by the accomplishments your friends remember that you have forgotten. Using the Personal Portrait and Wishes Profile can serve as a good focal point for your event. Add or delete relevant categories depending on the nature of your group.

You can be forthcoming about the purpose of the party, or you can mask the reason, making the exercise a game that is later revealed as a more practical and important exercise. Whichever way you choose to have your planning party, remember to have fun with it—it doesn't have to be serious. Here's an icebreaker that can help your guests get into the right mindset to plan: With everyone sitting in a circle, each person takes a turn guessing what the next person's (whom he or she doesn't know well) preferences are. For example, one guest says to the person next to her, "Your favorite kind of music is country; I could see you taking a vacation exploring the Amazon River; for a favorite meal, you would probably eat chicken pesto with orzo, arugula salad, and a full-bodied Barolo." Then that person tells everyone what he really likes, "I am hooked on Elvis Presley and music from the fifties; while I like the idea of going to the Amazon, my trip to the Pacific Northwest was awesome; I have always wanted to try Peking duck, would prefer an imported beer, and you can skip the green vegetables."

Another way to stimulate planning discussions might be to anonymously read selections from a completed Personal Portrait and Wishes Profile and ask the group to guess who wrote it. You might find it difficult to guess, or it might be very obvious. Either way, you will have a more complete and personal picture of your friends, and might also be inspired by their ideas enough to add them to your own profile.

Asking your friends to share their thoughts about the memorial services that they've attended can help you think more creatively about what you want for yours. Asking a few questions about what worked, what didn't, what was most memorable, or what you do and do not want is a simple and direct approach to generating ideas. You could also send an email message asking people to think of five things they want to be remembered for. Your conversations could inspire new and often surprising ideas.

IDEA 2: ANNIVERSARY PARTY

Sometimes it may be awkward to discuss a memorial service openly. There are many other ways, however, to glean the information you need to plan. For example, wedding anniversary parties—for your parents or other relatives—can be a good place to find information. By being observant and asking questions about their anniversary party, you can gather ideas that could make their memorial services more meaningful and personal.

When planning an anniversary party, or any type of celebration, always start big and then work toward attainable goals. Ask the honorees what they would want for a party if money were not a concern. Starting big and then working to what is feasible gives you a better picture of the honorees' true feelings and desires. Asking about their wedding ceremony is also a good way to gain perspective on the type of celebration the honorees might like. Helping to plan will also distinguish between what each honoree wants from the celebration. Taking the opportunity to get to know your parents' or loved ones' wishes for this celebration can reveal much about how they would like to be remembered. Here are some particular details to pay attention to:

- Who attended the party? (The guest list can often become the core group to call upon to help with the memorial service.)
- What was the venue and why was it chosen? Could you hold a reception or even the memorial service in the same place?
- What food and drink was served? Was there anything notable, unique, or personal about it?
- What were people wearing, and how formal was the event?

- Were there flowers? If so, why were they chosen?
- Did anyone give a speech or a toast, or recite a poem or a story? Pay attention to who spoke, what they said, and how well it was delivered. If possible, ask for a copy of anything you would like to remember or ask guests about their most memorable moments with the honorees.
- What kind of music was played? Were there special songs?
- Who was not invited? If family or friends were purposely excluded from this event (this can be tricky as you are not going to exclude anyone from the memorial service), then you will know not to have that person speaking or playing a prominent role at the memorial service.

Write down some notes and put them away in a safe place. After the party, ask the honorees how they felt about the celebration, what they did and did not like. You might even feel comfortable asking if they might like the same thing for their memorial service.

IDEA 3: SECOND MARRIAGE

If a couple gets married later in life, chances are their tastes are different than when they were younger. So take note of all the details of the wedding in the same way as you would for the anniversary party described above—you might want to incorporate these details into the memorial service. Remember that the people attending this wedding (as opposed to a first wedding, if there was one) will most likely also attend the memorial service. When planning a joint event, however, be careful to distinguish who likes what aspect of the event; weddings are often the result of many compromises. The memorial service presents an opportunity to eliminate compromise. It is a time for the surviving spouse to be magnanimous and adhere to the other's wishes, even if this requires you to provide the gentle reminder.

IDEA 4: EVENTS THAT HONOR SOMEONE

You can apply the same ideas you have learned from anniversary and other parties to other events. For example, a retirement party is a good opportunity to gather stories that are different from those relatives might tell.

You might also find a speaker for the memorial service, someone gratefully mentored, a favorite boss, or collaborating colleague. In the same way, award banquets can provide a different perspective on how a person should be remembered. The event itself might also serve as a way to add accomplishments to a eulogy or obituary. Chances are you will never attend the honoree's school reunion, but finding out who spoke, what stories were told, and learning about the honoree's old friends can give you insight into another aspect of the honoree's life.

It is important to highlight the diversity of experiences and people attending the memorial service. When thinking about speakers, try to include people who knew the honoree from different eras: school days, work life, volunteer effort, and the like.

IDEA 5: THE ROAST

A roast might seem like a perfect place to pick up important anecdotes and accolades, but it is important to remember that a memorial service is not a roast, and should never be in bad taste. Roasts are more often associated with retirement parties, but not always. They can also be given for someone who is moving, going back to school, or as a celebration for reaching a career pinnacle or goal.

Like other gatherings, attending a roast gives you the opportunity to learn more about the honoree's friends, hear more stories that may illuminate another side of the honoree's character, and maybe identify a good speaker. Even though some of the anecdotes told at a roast can be tasteless, you can always use more neutral elements of the story for the memorial service. These stories may not resonate with everyone, but for those who attended the roast (most likely a significant percentage of the honoree's friends and family), it may be meaningful to include some stories that only the insiders understand completely.

IDEA 6: FINANCIAL PLANNING PARTY

One way to take the dread out of preplanning your memorial service is to incorporate it with your other life-planning events. As people mature they begin to think more about financial, retirement, and estate planning. Financial planners are very willing to speak to groups, both to generate new clients and enhance trusted relationships with current ones. If you belong to a group you think might benefit from this type of discussion, consider inviting a financial planner to speak to them. When working with a financial planner, talk about how you wish to be remembered and what kind of living memorials you might want to leave behind: If you want to institute a named scholarship, who will be the administrator? Do you want to create a perpetual endowment fund? Maybe you want a park bench placed at a favorite spot or a plaque commemorating your donation to a hospital, or perhaps you prefer to give anonymously to your favorite charity. Many nonprofit institutions will meet with alumni, members, or supporters to provide them with assistance in creating a living memorial. Your financial planner will help ensure your financial wishes are funded and carried out adequately. During these planning sessions, do not forget to record important information in your Personal Portrait and Wishes Profile.

IDEA 7: WHEN NOT TO PLAN

This last idea is about when to avoid planning and identifying the times when no one will be receptive to it. Sometimes, celebrating perseverance is more important than preparing for the inevitable.

When one of my tennis friends found out that the love of her life had terminal cancer, maintaining a positive outlook became much more important than talking about planning a memorial service. I was planning a party a few months in advance that I wanted them to attend, and there was something so positive about including them, even though the future was uncertain. And when they *both* attended the party, the focus was more on a celebration of survival than anything else. Was there even a remote connection between the party and a memorial service? No, and there shouldn't have been.

My oncologist sister observes that hearing is the last of the senses to fail before people die. Yet many times loved ones gather around the bedside to say good-bye and start talking about the funeral, the inheritance, the house, or the speakers at the service, before their loved one is gone. Here is another time where planning is best left undone. Please remember that it is very possible that everything you say can be heard even though someone may appear unconscious or unresponsive.

Someone who is facing death may one minute talk about no longer buying green bananas or new shoes. The next day, the same person might buy a new fur coat or a lifetime membership to a national park. Be sensitive to where the people are with their own process of acceptance, and do not push preparations if the time does not seem right. Similarly, when people have just gone through a life-threatening event, they may have a renewed sense of life and what they might still want to accomplish. They may not be in a frame of mind to express their wishes for a memorial service, and it may be best not to pressure them.

HELPFUL RESOURCES

The websites and resources listed in this appendix are not an endorsement of their respective services. Individuals should perform their own due diligence when accessing information, advice, or services to ensure it is accurate and trustworthy.

Balloon releases

Balloon Release FAQ:
www.balloonrelease.com

Balloon Release Guidelines:
www.nabas.co.uk/balloon.html

Butterfly release

Live Monarch:
www.livemonarch.com

Swallowtail Farms:
www.butterflyrelease.org

Clip art

DoverPublications.com:
store.doverpublications.com

Eulogies

Prewritten Eulogies:
www.heartfelteulogies.com

Flags

www.flagstuff.com

Gravestone Symbols

Cemetery Symbols:
www.buffaloah.com/a/forestL/symbols

Symbolism in the Carvings on Old Gravestones:
www.genevahistoricalsociety.com/PDFs/Cemetery%20Stories/Symbol%20List.pdf

Symbols from Various Cultures:
alsirat.com/symbols/symbols1.html

Traditional Christian Symbols:
histpres.mtsu.edu/then/cemetery/page3.html

Mementos

Bookmarks:
www.printingforless.com

Postcards:
www.psprint.com
www.amazingmail.com

Custom T-Shirts:
www.shirtmagic.com

Obituaries

Baranick, Alana. *Life on the Death Beat: A Handbook for Obituary Writers*. New York: Marion Street Press, Inc., 2005.

Johnson, Marilyn. *The Dead Beat: Lost Souls, Lucky Stiffs, and the Perverse Pleasures of Obituaries.* New York: HarperCollins, 2006.

Obituary How-To:
www.lippertfuneralhome.com/owg.htm

Programs for the Service
Buy Templates for Funeral Programs:
www.funeralprinter.com

Funeral Program Templates for MS Publisher:
family-heritage-templates.com/memorial_program_booklet.htm

Secular Celebrations
Secular Celebrants:
www.secularhumanism.org/library/shb/celebrants_14_1.html

Secular Celebrations:
www.secular-celebrations.com

Sheet Music and Lyrics
2 Free Downloads Per Day:
www.sheetmusicarchive.net

Online Sheet Music Store:
www.sheetmusicplus.com

Sheet Music Downloads:
www.sheetmusicdirect.com

Symbols
Meanings of Heraldic Symbols:
www.fleurdelis.com/meanings.htm

Mourning Imagery:
members.aol.com/TombView/symbol2.html

Symbols of the Saints in Art:
www.fisheaters.com/saintsart.html

Symbols of Traditional Cultures
Chinese Lanterns:
www.chinavoc.com/festivals/ghost.htm

Totem Pole Meanings:
www.chainsawsculptors.com/totem_poles.htm

White Dove Release
White Dove Release Directory of America:
www.awdra.com

White Dove Release Professionals:
www.white-dove-releases.com

Wire Easels
Baltimore Display Industries:
www.bdisales.com

Potomac Display:
www.potomacdisplay.com

ACKNOWLEDGMENTS

My gratitude goes to Claudia Gere, who came into my life and helped me create this book in a magical way that makes me miss our time working together. Her patient author coaching, research, savvy editing, and knowledgeable book proposal writing made the difference between an idea in my head and the completed book you hold in your hand.

I also thank my research assistants, Caitlin Freeman and Allan Denchfield, who provided copious notes, websites, and facts that helped provide content for the reference sections. Jane Forsyth, Lindy Hess, Cathy Hemming, and Phoebe Leed were enthusiastic and encouraging from the get-go and provided all-important logistical support. Jim Evans was single handedly responsible for maintaining an outstanding quality of life in our little household as we neared the finish line, and for this I am eternally grateful.

INDEX

Published in 2009 by Stewart, Tabori & Chang
An imprint of Harry N. Abrams, Inc.

Text copyright © 2009 Faith Moore

Library of Congress Cataloging-in-Publication Data:
Moore, Faith.
 Celebrating a life: planning memorial services and other creative
remembrances / Faith Moore.
   p. cm.
 ISBN 978-1-58479-765-4
 1. Memorial service. I. Title.
 BV199.M4M66 2009
 393'.9--dc22
 2008052275

Editor: Ann Stratton
Designer: Jen Cogliantry
Production Manager: Tina Cameron

Stewart, Tabori & Chang books are available at special discounts when
purchased in quantity for premiums and promotions as well as fundraising
or educational use. Special editions can also be created to specification. For
details, contact specialmarkets@hnabooks.com or write to the address below.

Printed and bound in the United States of America
10 9 8 7 6 5 4 3 2 1

HNA

harry n. abrams, inc.

a subsidiary of La Martinière Groupe

115 West 18th Street
New York, NY 10011
www.hnabooks.com